How to Write
Your Life
Story
in Ten Easy Steps

Visit our How To website at www.howto.co.uk

At www.howto.co.uk you can engage in conversation with our authors – all of whom have 'been there and done that' in their specialist fields. You can get access to special offers and additional content but most importantly you will be able to engage with, and become a part of, a wide and growing community of people just like yourself.

At www.howto.co.uk you'll be able to talk and share tips with people who have similar interests and are facing similar challenges in their lives. People who, just like you, have the desire to change their lives for the better – be it through moving to a new country, starting a new business, growing their own vegetables, or writing a novel.

At www.howto.co.uk you'll find the support and encouragement you need to help make your aspirations a reality.

You can go direct to www.writing-your-life-story-in-ten-easy-steps.co.uk which is part of the main How To site.

How To Books strives to present authentic, inspiring, practical information in their books. Now, when you buy a title from **How To Books,** you get even more than just words on a page.

How to Write
Your Life
Story

in Ten Easy Steps

Sophie King

howtobooks

Published by How To Books Ltd,
Spring Hill House, Spring Hill Road,
Begbroke, Oxford OX5 1RX
Tel: (01865) 375794. Fax: (01865) 379162
info@howtobooks.co.uk
www.howtobooks.co.uk

How To Books greatly reduce the carbon footprint of their books by sourcing their typesetting and printing in the UK.

British Library Cataloguing in Publication Data
A catalogue record for this book is available from the British Library

ISBN: 978 1 84528 407 7

Produced for How To Books by Deer Park Productions, Tavistock
Typeset by PDQ Typesetting Ltd, Staffordshire
Printed and bound in Great Britain by Bell & Bain Ltd, Glasgow

NOTE: The material contained in this book is set out in good faith for general guidance and no liability can be accepted for loss or expense incurred as a result of relying in particular circumstances on statements made in the book. The laws and regulations are complex and liable to change, and readers should check the current position with the relevant authorities before making personal arrangements.

Contents

STEP EIGHT HOW TO END YOUR LIFE STORY – AND MAKE SURE THAT IT DOESN'T HURT ANYONE (INCLUDING YOURSELF)

STEP NINE HOW TO PRESENT YOUR LIFE STORY AND GET IT PUBLISHED

STEP TEN STILL STUCK? TRIED AND TESTED REMEDIES

Introduction

'My life would make a book!'

How often have you said that? Or heard it said? And the truth is, that it probably would. In my experience as a journalist and novelist, it's not the lives of celebrities that are page-turners. No. It's the extraordinary lives of ordinary people. The sort of people that you probably know. Your milkman who used to be a bank manager. Your elderly neighbour who worked for the Resistance movement during the war. The woman at the end of the computer help desk who, unknown to you, is looking after her aged father, four children and doing an OU degree.

All of these people (whom I've actually come across in real life) have tales to tell about their lives that would make you laugh. And make you cry. But the best part about them is that they are all true. And because of that, they are inspirations to us all.

But there's one person we haven't mentioned in that list above. Someone you know very well. So well that you might think they are actually pretty boring even though they might be fascinating to everyone else.

That's right. YOU.

But why, you might be thinking, should you bother to write your own life story? Wouldn't everyone else be bored by it and isn't it a rather boastful thing to do, considering you're not rich and famous?

Actually, that's not true. There are, I believe, three very good reasons for writing your life story. First, it leaves a precious gift for your children and grandchildren or any other relatives who might want to know – after you've gone – what happened in your life. After all, how often have you yourself wished you'd listened more to your own mother or father or well-meaning relative who bored you as a child or young adult, with tales of 'the old days'? The chances are that you only listened with one ear and now that Mother or Father or relative has died, you can't remember exactly what they said. This becomes particularly poignant when you have your own children and suddenly get the same craving that your own parents will have had, when they wanted to pass down a piece of history so that it would continue to live in family folklore. But unless you have written down all those stories that you were told, you won't be able to do that. Even verbal accounts can become distorted (one of my cousins, for instance, who was 'discovered' by his father in Malaysia 40 years ago, has been given four different versions of how this happened and isn't sure which one to believe). But if someone has bothered to write down their life story, we will know as far as possible what really happened.

Second, writing your life story can be a fantastic way for you to make sense of your own life. You can look back on the things you did and, from that, decide how to live the rest of your time. One of my students who is in prison (I'm currently writer in residence of a high security prison) recently wrote his 50,000 word life story. 'It made me remember things I'd blanked out in my mind,' he told me. 'And I realised how many wrong decisions I'd made. I'm going to change all that now.'

It's not just prisoners who feel this. Another of my students is a very pretty divorcee with two marriages behind her. She was also imprisoned in a concentration camp during the war when a teenager. This student came to me to write her life story because she wanted to 'release the demons' by writing about events which she couldn't talk about to friends and family.

By the end of the six-month period during which I helped her ghost her life story, she began to feel more at ease with herself. Why? Because it was plain to anyone who read it that she was a survivor rather than just a victim or someone who had been dealt an unfair hand in life. 'That boosted my confidence,' she said. 'I'm going to see myself differently from now on.' I hope she did because the funny thing is that when you see yourself differently, so do others – because you start to act differently and demand respect rather than attracting put-downs.

The third reason to write a life story is that you are guaranteed to get it published – not necessarily by a publisher who will pay you. But by someone who you might pay instead. This can cost as little as a few pounds down at the local printers if you simply type it up and get it bound. Alternatively, you could pay up to £500 (or a lot less) and end up with a hard-cover book. Or you could publish it free on the net. Either way, you will end up with a book, which isn't necessarily the case if you write a novel and try to get someone else to publish it.

Finally, there's one more reason to get that pen out or switch on the keyboard. And that is that many writers who chronicle their life stories find inspiration for writing something else afterwards. It might be a novel or a short story or perhaps a poem. Because once you've started writing, you'll get the habit. Trust me. And trust yourself. Here goes! You're going to have the time of your life!

Step One

How to Begin

Who do you think you are? 1

INTRODUCING YOURSELF TO YOUR FUTURE READERSHIP

The exciting thing about beginning your life story is that you don't know who is going to end up reading it. It might be a future great-grandchild who will never have met you. It could be a grown-up son or daughter who seizes on your life story because it brings back precious memories of you. It could be a complete stranger who picks it up at an auction or whatever the equivalent will be in a hundred years' time. Or it could be a relative or friend who reads it while you are still alive and well, just because they are interested in what went on in your life before they knew you.

But whoever your readership is, you need to start your first chapter in the same way that you would if you were introducing yourself to someone. In other words, you should begin with your name and essential facts about yourself. This might feel a bit odd at first and even rather pretentious. After all, who do you think you are? But the truth is that because you don't know who will be reading this, it's vital to get the facts straight at the beginning.

WHAT EXACTLY SHOULD YOU SAY?

What's in a name?

Begin as you would if you met yourself at a party. In other words, with your name! But this is where it gets fun. If you have a middle name or names, give them too and – even better – if they have a family significance, explain why.

Many people have relatives' names as their middle names and often, there can be a story in that. For instance, one of my sons has 'Alastair Romer' as his two middle names. 'Alastair' is after my eldest uncle who is now dead, but when he was 17 he lied about his age in order to get into the RAF during the Second World War. He had, in fact, promised his mother (my grandmother) that he wouldn't fight, but when she died of cancer at the tender age of 41 during the war, he considered himself exonerated from that promise. He was then shot down by the Germans over Norway where he was hidden by locals until word got out that the Germans would shoot anyone harbouring the 'enemy'. My Uncle Alastair then gave himself up because he didn't want anyone to be hurt and spent the rest of the war in a concentration camp. My mother (his sister), who was nine when her mother died, didn't know if her brother was alive or dead until the end of the war. Meanwhile, 'Romer' is a family name which takes in gypsies and judges. So you can see that middle names can be a story in themselves. . .

JANE'S STORY

‘*My middle name is Betty. I am always having to tell officials that it's not short for 'Elizabeth'. It's actually Betty on my birth certificate because that's what my grandmother was called. I didn't know her because she had died before I was born. But it makes me feel closer to her by having her name as mine. When I wrote my life story, I talked about that. The funny thing was that my daughter didn't even know what her great-grandmother was called until she read it and then, when her daughter was born, she decided to christen her Betty. I was thrilled because it continued family tradition. But if she hadn't read my life story, that might not have happened.*’

Date and place of birth

After your name, the next important fact is when you were born. If possible, include the time of your birth. If you don't know – and many of us don't – ask surviving relatives if they have any idea when this was. Or see if your mother kept a Baby Record book (which is where I found out mine). Why is this important? Basically, the more detail you can put in, the more your life story will literally come to life. And if your relatives are into astrology, they might want to work out your star chart in relation to theirs. It might also be that they were born at a similar time of the year. My father casually mentioned that his father – my deceased grandfather – had a birthday which was only two days after mine. It gave me a funny feeling. . .

The place of your birth will be on your birth certificate (see the following chapters on research). Again, this could be really fascinating for future readers. It might be that they themselves have personal links with that place, which will make it more special. Or it could be a vital fact for them if they are researching the family tree.

STEVEN'S STORY

' *When my wife's uncle wrote his life story, I found out that he had grown up in the same part of Yorkshire as my grandparents. They hadn't known each other but it was an amazing coincidence which we'd never have discovered. And it's been a good talking point when we've got together at family occasions.* '

Your family

Your introduction to your life story also needs to describe your immediate family. This might include your:

+ parents;
+ husband/wife/partner;
+ children;
+ grandchildren;
+ brothers/sisters;
+ nieces/nephews.

Make sure you say how old they are at the time of writing and what they do and where they live. You might like to include a small pen sketch of what they are like. For instance, perhaps your sister loves cats. Maybe your brother is a film buff.

You could also bring them to life with small anecdotes. Perhaps your brother gave you away at your wedding and made a funny speech. Maybe your youngest child is learning the violin and driving you mad with the noise! A life story needs to include laughter. Like any book, you want to engage the reader's attention and make them feel involved with your characters.

Also give some facts about your relatives.

- How old are they?
- What do they do?
- Where do they live?
- Do you see them often?

Your own vital statistics

Not those kind of statistics! But you do need to mention the following:

- your job
- where you live now
- how you spend your time – it might help here to describe a typical day, if there is such a thing
- what you like and dislike (this could be food preferences or certain films)
- pets
- favourite songs/books/favourite anything
- hobbies/talents
- ambitions
- hopes/fears – be honest about these last two categories
- list of favourites. Write down a list of your favourite things: favourite meal; favourite poem; favourite television programme; favourite shops; favourite book; favourite outfit; favourite hobby; favourite sport, etc. If possible, give a short reason about why you like it.

Bring in as much detail as you can in this section. It will make you come alive to whoever reads it. Just imagine if you were living in the future and discovered that your great-aunt enjoyed playing rugby for an all-girls' team. It would make you think of her in a new light. . .

Mini blog and picture

Write your own CV – including both facts and emotional aspects too. Include:

- basic information about yourself such as where you live;
- what you hope to do in life;
- what your job is and where you hope to be in ten years' time;
- what you look like (if you find this hard to do, get a friend to describe you);
- what you are most proud of;
- what you are most ashamed of;
- awards;
- a current picture of yourself and one when you were younger.

The latter is really important. Think how you feel when looking back through pictures of relatives. It's fascinating to see how they dress and what they look like. Well, that's how future relatives will think when they see your picture – except that yours will be different! You could say what you were doing at the time; where you were; and who was in the picture with you. There's nothing more infuriating than looking at old photographs and wondering who was with your great-aunt or grandmother. But your picture will have a caption to make it clear. Fascinating. . .

Current world events
Tell your unknown reader what is going on in the world at the moment. This will create a vivid time capsule. Illustrate it if possible with clippings from current local papers.

WHY YOU ARE WRITING THIS

This is your chance to explain why you are writing your life story. You might want to explain that you are doing it to preserve family memories. And maybe you could suggest that future family members write their own life stories too!

Remember this is an introduction. It's a brief outline about yourself as a person, designed to whet the appetite of the person who has picked it up. So I would suggest dividing it into sections, just like this chapter, with similar headings. For instance, you could begin with the heading 'WHY I'M WRITING MY LIFE STORY'. Write a few paragraphs (maybe half a page) about what gave you the idea. Then you could follow this up with another section, headed 'WHAT I'M CALLED'. In this section, you could give your name and middle names as well as any family relevance. After that, 'MY FAMILY' and then a paragraph on why you are writing your life story.

Aim for about half a page in each section and do try to type it up or else ask someone else to do it for you.

Alternatively, you could write a shorter introduction, called something like 'ALL ABOUT ME!' and include all the information we've just discussed. That will bring you to the end of Chapter 1!

EXAMPLE OF AN INTRODUCTION

My name is Henry Smith and I am 63 at the time of writing (2010). I live in London and have two grown-up children and four grandchildren. I grew up in Stanmore but spent most of my married life in south London where I have continued to live after the death of my wife. I enjoy reading and an occasional round of golf.

I used to work as an engineer but now I am retired. I enjoy model making. I also like looking round boat yards and visiting old ships like the *Mary Rose*. In the evenings, I sometimes watch quiz shows on television such as *Mastermind* or listen to Radio 4.

I have one sister, Mary, who now lives in Toronto. I visited her for the first time last year and hope to do so again next year.

My favourite meal is pork chops and mashed potato!

At the moment, the British Prime Minister is David Cameron and the President of the United States is Barack Obama.

I am writing my life story because my grandchildren are all young at the moment and not very interested in the stories I have told them about my life. I am hoping that one day they will want to know what the world was like when I was growing up, so I want to leave this book behind me, when I die, as a sort of 'This Was My Life'.

SUMMARY

- ◆ Start off with an explanation about why you're writing your life story.
- ◆ Then introduce yourself. Do this by outlining your:
  - names;
  - place of birth and date of birth;
  - astrological sign;
  - details about family;
  - job details or how you spend your time;
  - list of favourites (food, television programmes, etc.).

Step Two

Using the Power of Memory

Do you remember when? 2

USING MEMORIES TO WRITE YOUR LIFE STORY

Fantastic! You now have the material and ideas to write Chapter 1 – the introduction to yourself. But where do you go from here?

The first step is to use the material that is already in your head: your memories. After all, if you want to get an older person talking, all you have to do is ask them about what they remember from the past. Anyone over the age of 30 (roughly!) loves talking about things they 'used to do', whether they enjoyed them or not. You'll get all sorts of stories such as the day they first started a new job or how they met their partner or the kind of food that their mother would cook when they were little.

And although you might find this a bit boring at the time, the irony is that it's memories like these which become far more important and exciting when that person is no longer alive to tell you about them.

That's the sad part...The good news is that you are still around to think about your **own** memories and this book is going to show you how to present them in a way that will entertain its future readers.

Buy yourself a bound book with ruled pages. Use this as your Research Book and begin by writing down some of the memories which you're going to get after reading this chapter.

YOUR FIRST MEMORY

When I teach my students how to write their life stories, I ask them to think of the first thing they can remember as a child. Some people go completely blank. Others will have a very vivid picture of a scene that stands out in their mind. And some will have a vague idea of a place but not sure where it is.

The truth is that no one can be certain that something is their very **first** memory. But if we try hard enough with the right tools, you can be prompted into recalling something that made an impact on you in your early years. So if you belong to the first group, when you can't think of anything, don't panic! I'll be giving you some pointers.

If you have an extremely vivid picture of a scene, you might either have a fantastic memory or you could be recalling something which happened when you were older than you thought. You might even be linking different scenes in your mind from different occasions. But it doesn't matter! What is more important is that you have a clear picture of that scene in your head.

Even if you can't – in other words, if you belong to the dim and distant memory brigade – a vague picture can be intriguing. Take one of my students who wrote about this memory:

'*I'm sitting on a beach, playing with stones. I think – but I'm not sure – that I'm trying to build them up into a tower but every time I reach a certain height, they fall down. Someone bends down to help me (I think it's my mother) but I don't want her to help me and I feel cross with her.*'

When my student tried to find out more about her memory, she was told by her parents that they only once took her to the sea when she was a child – and that was when she was 18 months' old. They were, however, able to tell her that they took her to a beach near Exmouth that was indeed stony, although they didn't remember her building a tower of stones! But my student's mother was able to find some old black and white photographs that showed the family on the beach – and lo and behold, there was a picture of my student building a stone sandcastle with the help of her mother! She was then able to use that photograph in her life story.

TRIGGERS TO HELP RELEASE EARLY MEMORIES

If you're not able to recall many memories, it might help to think of some trigger events. The following are often useful:

Birthdays Can you remember a birthday party when you were small? It might be yours or it might be someone else's.

KATRINA'S MEMORY

'*I remember going to a fancy dress party and my mother dressed me up as a daisy. I wore a ballet tutu and had a little wire head dress that she'd made for me. I still recall how excited and special I felt when we walked along the street to my friend's house.*'

Christmas This is usually a good one. It probably won't be your first Christmas – you'd need a pretty good memory to recall that one! But dig deeply and you will probably remember an early one.

PETER'S MEMORY

'*I remember getting into a door in a London department store called Gamages that has shut now, and feeling very excited because we were suddenly on a sort of train! It went round several corners (at least, it did in my memory) and then we got out to meet a large gentleman in red. I was convinced it was Father Christmas himself. But I'm not sure what happened after that.*'

In fact, something DID – Peter burst into tears! – but he couldn't remember that. It was only when Peter, who is now in his forties, mentioned it to his sister that she filled in the gaps. Relatives and friends can be very helpful about recalling blanks; but more of that in the following chapters on research.

Holidays. Anything out of the ordinary should trigger off memories. When describing your memory, try to include colours, smells and noises.

JILL'S MEMORY

'*I clearly remember being woken up in the middle of the night by my mother who said we were going on holiday. I don't remember being told where (although I now know it was Cornwall) but I do recall having to wash and get dressed when it was still dark outside. It was both scary and exciting. The funny thing is that I remember more about getting ready for the holiday than the holiday itself which is a bit of a blank. But I can see in my head the bathroom where I washed in the night at home, before leaving. It had black and white diamond tiles. Very 1950s!*'

Details like this can make a memory come alive! Those black and white diamond tiles probably strike chords with a lot of us. And in fact it doesn't matter that Jill can't remember the holiday; in a way, the getting ready for the journey is more powerful than a standard account of a trip to the beach.

Birth of siblings (brothers/sisters) This usually gets people thinking! As psychologists tell us, we go through all kind of emotions ranging from jealousy to excitement and a mixture of both when a baby brother or sister is born. If this applies to you, try to recall your feelings and also atmospheric details that describe the period. Here's an example below:

BETTY'S MEMORY

'*I remember staying with my friend Susan which was a real treat. We were having breakfast and I was just cracking open the top of a boiled egg – I can still see the pattern of the dining room chair I was sitting on – and my friend's mother came into the room. She had a big smile on her face. "You've got a baby sister!" she said.*

Even now, I can still feel a mixture of confusion and excitement. I knew I ought to be pleased from the look on my friend's mother's face. But I also remember feeling a bit upset that I had to leave my boiled egg and walk down the road with my friend's mother to see my baby sister. She was in my parents' big bed next to my mother and the room was dark inside. When I went in, there was a loud scream and it hurt my ears. My mother wanted me to go up and say hello but I stayed at the door because of the noise.

There were telegrams on the table next to my mother. One had a picture of a big yellow stork.'

The great thing about this memory is that it combines a young child's emotions with contemporary descriptions. Telegrams in the early 1960s, where this memory came from, were often sent for happy occasions, as well as a way of communicating something urgent.

I also like the use of dialogue in my student's memory here when she shows what her friend's mother said, in speech marks. This makes it come alive.

Another great point about memories relating to births of brothers or sisters is that you can date that memory. Betty's sister was born in January 1961, so she can pinpoint that memory exactly and know that she herself was six years old at the time.

First day at school We're not expecting miracles here! After all, it's highly unlikely that you're going to remember the very first day at school. But you might well remember something about one of the first days you were there. Any new experience tends to stand out in our minds and school is surely one of them. The funny thing is that we don't always remember the sort of things we think we should, such as what the teacher was like or what the other children did or said. Instead, we frequently recall seemingly irrelevant details such as the one below. But the good thing about this is that it's these kind of details which make your account stand as unique to your own life story.

MIRIAM'S LIFE STORY
' *When I tried to think about my early memories, I came up with a picture of a sunny, glass building in my head. There was mustard and cress on the window sill, growing out of*

pink blotting paper. I don't recall having any feelings about that – just that it was there. But it was the soap in the wash basins that I really remember because I didn't like the smell. I also remember dancing round the room to music.

When I did some research by asking other members of my family about what I was like when I was little, my mother told me that she was worried when I first started school because I began blinking a lot. Then she went to a parents' evening and found that one of my teachers blinked very rapidly when she spoke. It turned out that I was copying her!

Favourite toys   Most children have a special teddy and maybe a doll as well. Perhaps they also had a special toy that meant a lot to them and that, as a result, forms an important part of their childhood memories. Many adults still have that toy – sometimes hidden in a cupboard – and that gives this memory an even more special significance if someone finds it after you're gone, and realises from your life story that it meant a lot to you.

ROBERT'S MEMORY

'I had a teddy that went everywhere with me, including hospital where I was admitted at the age of three with pneumonia. It sounds a bit wet now but I do remember not wanting to eat a plate of mince in hospital. As a punishment, one of the nurses put my bear on top of a wardrobe in the room and I cried my eyes out.'

That story makes my eyes prick with tears too! It shows how different things were in those days – at least, I hope they are. But clearly, that incident had a profound effect on Robert who is now in his late fifties but still remembers it.

Pets   A family pet is part of the family – and continues to live on in memory for years afterwards. Did you have a pet?

ANGIE'S MEMORY

'We had a small dog called Roger who always slept on my bed. He was my friend and I told him everything. One day, he went missing and I was heartbroken. Even my father – who

was always shouting at him – was upset. Then we got a phone call from the police station to say someone had handed him in. As soon as we got Roger home, my father bought him a large steak as a treat because we were so relieved to have him back. That was in 1972. I remember the date because the year after that, my brother went to university.'

TRIGGERS FOR LATER MEMORIES

Hopefully, you've now got quite a few memories written down. Some of them might make you feel a bit sad, like Robert's. In fact, that is something you need to be aware of when writing your life story. It can remind you of incidents that you had forced yourself to block out. Some therapists might argue that it is helpful to write down your memories but, if you are finding it very painful, you might want to move on to Chapter 20 for guidance.

Meanwhile, I'd like you to continue if you want, and think of some more memories to add to your list in your Life Story Book. They can be memories from any time in your life. It doesn't matter if they're big or small! Just write them down with as much detail as possible and, later in the book, I will give you some ideas on how to use them.

Films Do you remember a film that moved you? Think about why it affected you. Who were you with? What stage of your life were you at?

PAT'S FILM MEMORY

'*I went to see* That'll Be The Day *when I was 17 with a boy called Colin. I didn't think I liked him very much but I did want to see the film so when he asked me, I went! In fact, we got on better than I had thought we would and went out for four years after that. Every time I read about David Essex, who starred in the film, I think of my boyfriend Colin.*'

Television It's amazing what an impact television pro-grammes had on us. I personally used to love *Bill and Ben* and also the *Wooden Tops*. Here's another memory:

HELEN'S TV MEMORY

'*I used to love* The Avengers *but it was after my bedtime (I think I was about 11 at the time). Sometimes, I would beg my mother to let me stay up late and watch it even though it scared me!*'

Clothes   Now here's a good one to bring back those memories! Here are some prompters from some of my life story students that might help you think of some of your own.

LESLEY'S FASHION MEMORY

'*I used to love clothes shopping at Chelsea Girl because it was dark inside – that was part of its charm. In the sixties.*'

ANNIE'S FASHION MEMORY

'*I still have a pair of Mary Quant stockings in their packet which I bought when they were at the height of fashion in the sixties. I also have a photograph of me wearing 'hot pants'. They were silvery blue and very popular!*'

Pocket money   You might not remember exactly how much you got – but then again, you might remember what you bought with it.

TERESA'S POCKET MONEY

'*I used to get my pocket money every Saturday. I would save it up, like all my friends, and buy something special – often for family birthdays. I remember buying my mother a china salt and pepper set which I still have, now she's dead. I'll always remember the pleasure on her face when I gave it to her – and the nice warm feeling it gave me.*'

Bedrooms   A child's bedroom is a special private space which often brings back memories, even if it had to be shared with a sibling. Here are some stories:

TOM'S BEDROOM MEMORIES

'*I had a bedroom of my own until my brother was born when I was four. Then, presumably when he was older, we were given bunk beds. That was very exciting. I bagged the*

*top one and would sit on the top and look out over our street.
I felt like a captain of a ship!'*

Friends   Most of us remember our friends and even better,
we might have pictures of them.

BILLY'S FRIEND MEMORY

*' I used to be great friends with two other boys in our street.
We would go everywhere together – football in the park was
the best! Even now, at the age of 60 odd, we meet up and we
still have the occasional kick around!'*

Zoo/other days out   Do you remember going to the zoo or
a museum or having a helter skelter ride? What was it like?
How did it feel? Who did you go with?

ALEXA'S ZOO MEMORY

*' When I was a Girl Guide, we all went to a zoo. I'm not sure
where it was but it had a ghost ride at the end with some
amusement arcades. It was the ghost ride, rather than the
animals, that I remember! It was also exciting going with
friends on a bus with the other guides and not being with our
parents. That's reminded me! The following summer, I went
camping with the guides in Sussex (I can't remember where
exactly). It was really good fun even though it rained every
day!'*

Alcohol   This might be one memory you'd rather not
remember! But it certainly seems to trigger a few stories for
some

MAGGIE'S DRINK MEMORY

*' The first time I had an alcoholic drink was when I was 15
and someone gave me a glass of cider at a party. When I got
home, I was a bit tipsy and my mum was cross. It put me off
drink and I didn't have another "proper drink" until I went
to university and discovered cheap white wine! Sounds crazy
now, doesn't it?'*

Try to remember the funny bits to inject some humour into your life story. If you can make your reader laugh, you're more likely to involve them and get them interested.

There are several other triggers you could use to recall memories, but I want to save them for later chapters – especially those in Chapter 9 when I will be showing you how you can structure your life story around 'Firsts'. For instance, you could have a page about 'First drink'; a page about 'First love'; a page about 'First Home' and so on.

In the meantime, keep writing those memories down!

HOW TO USE YOUR MEMORIES IN YOUR LIFE STORY

There are two ways of doing this.

1. Either you can write the memories down as a list and then use them as part of your research to paint a fuller picture (I'll be giving you ideas on how to do this in the following chapters).

2. Or you can use the memories themselves as a framework for your life story. For instance, you could divide the book into short sections, with each chapter having a memory heading. You might have AN EARLY MEMORY; A MEMORY FROM EARLY CHILDHOOD; A MEMORY FROM MY TEENAGE YEARS; A MEMORY OF MY FIRST JOB and so on. Under each section, you could then describe what you remember in as much detail as possible (see Chapter 5).

However, at this stage, I suggest you write down all your memories in your Research Book and keep your options open on how you are going to use them. The important thing is that you've caught some of them by writing them down. So now they won't be lost for ever...

SUMMARY

- Start by writing down an early memory.
- Include any noises, colours, smells or any other senses that go with that memory.
- Describe any emotions that you felt at the time (if you remember them) such as: anger; happiness; fear; excitement.
- Try to remember who you were with at the time.
- Look for photographs that go with that memory.
- Think of triggers that might help you recall memories. For example:
  - birthdays
  - holidays
  - birth of brothers/sisters
  - pets
  - Christmas
  - bedrooms
  - school.
- Continue to think of other triggers for later memories such as, films; TV; clothes; special outings.

Step Three

How to Start Your Research

Researching the spoken word 3

You may have lots of stories about your life in your head right now, which you are itching to write down. And that's great! But your life story will be so much better if you also take the trouble to do some research and dig up anecdotes that you didn't know about before.

Chapters 3 and 4 are going to show you how to start your research. Chapter 3 will concentrate on the spoken word and Chapter 4 on how to research from documents of different kinds. Make sure you have plenty of pens, pencils and a hard-backed notebook so pages don't get lost. It might also help to have a Dictaphone so you can record what people tell you instead of – or as well as – writing it down.

TALKING TO LIVING RELATIVES

Make a list of everyone who is still alive and who has known you for part – or all of – your life. Include family friends as well as relatives. Begin with people who knew you as a child. It's best to do it this way because it will help you think of your life story in a chronological way, which will make it easier to structure.

There's also another – rather sobering – reason for beginning with people who knew you as a child and that is that they may well be elderly themselves so they might not have too long to live. In fact, you might find that talking to older relatives about the past has unexpected benefits.

Susan, a life story student of mine, always used to visit her great-uncle once a year.

'*It was a bit of an ordeal especially as my children were young and would run round the house which was embarrassing. But one year, I visited my great-uncle on my own and explained that I was researching my life story and that I wondered if he could remember anything about me as a child. He got quite excited about the project and we ended up talking for hours. He told me all kinds of things I didn't know such as the fact that my mother (who is now dead) almost married someone else instead of my father. Although that wasn't strictly my own life story, it was part of my background because she married my dad a year later and then had me, ten months after that! So I was able to make a joke about it in my life story and say that if she hadn't changed her mind, I wouldn't have been born!*'

Feel awkward?

You might feel a bit embarrassed about contacting friends and relatives with a view to speaking about yourself. So why not say you're doing some general family research and also ask them questions about their life too. It might add some general colour and it would certainly be interesting for future readers.

Brian started writing his life story last year.

'*I have a step-father who is a very quiet man. He started to bring me up when I was three and my father died. I began by asking him about his own childhood and realised, as he was talking, that I had never bothered asking him much about his life before. He seemed to be very pleased and described how his father was a steam engine driver and used to let him stand in the front of the train and shovel coal on the furnace. Then I asked him how he met my mother. Although I already knew they were introduced by friends, I hadn't realised that it was at a tea dance. After that, he told me that my mother didn't want to introduce him to me until she knew they were going to be serious. I didn't know any of this from my own mother; she hadn't told me (presumably she felt it wasn't right to talk to a child about this) and she is now in a home with senile dementia so isn't able to remember much. My stepfather said that when he first met me, I was very interested in wildlife. So he brought me some tadpoles and when they got bigger we put*' *them in a pond. I don't remember any of this but it made me feel closer to him than I had as a child. It also made a nice anecdote for my life story.*'

Good questions to ask

Not everyone is a natural interviewer! You might find it easier to talk to a relative about what you were like as a child if you have a list of questions to hand. Below are some examples.

- How old was I when you first saw me?
- What did I look like?
- Did I look like anyone else in the family?
- Was I the first boy/girl to be born for several years?
- What kind of baby was I (contented; always crying, etc.)?
- What was my bedroom like?
- Can you remember – and describe – big events in my life as I grew up, e.g. christening; birthday parties; holidays?
- Do you remember anything funny that I did?
- Or something naughty?

What does your relative remember about:

- your school (maybe one of the relatives took you to school one day);
- Christmases/birthdays;
- thank you letters that you wrote;
- houses that you lived in;
- stories about you and your parents;
- stories about you and cousins/sisters/brothers;
- confirmation (if you were confirmed);
- your friends;
- holidays;
- big events in the family that might have affected you;
- anything else at all?

Having a list of questions is very useful. But a good interviewer also listens carefully to the answers and then adapts their next question accordingly. For instance, you might ask an aunt if she remembers the first time she saw you as a baby and what her impressions were. She might reply that you were a happy contented child, although you didn't like being left with other people. Over to you, now, to ask her for examples of this. Did the aunt look after you when your mother went away? Where did she go? How did the aunt manage? It's anecdotes like this that make a life story come alive.

Annie, another of my students, discovered that an aunt had looked after her for a week when she was six and her mother had to go into hospital.

'*According to my aunt, I was very difficult until she hit on a great way of keeping me amused. Making gingerbread! The funny thing is that I love cooking now and hadn't realised it had come from my aunt who got me started! That was something I was able to put in my life story.*'

WHAT TO PUT IN – AND WHAT TO LEAVE OUT

Sometimes, relatives and friends will tell you things you didn't know – and which might be upsetting. Take Shauna's story:

'*My Godmother told me that my parents had got married when my mother was three months pregnant with me. I didn't know that before and although I was in my late forties when she told me (because I was 'interviewing' her for my life story), it made me feel uncomfortable. My parents hadn't had a particularly happy marriage. Would they have got married if it hadn't been for me? Although my parents are still alive, it's not a question I feel I can ask them – or indeed tell them that I know they 'had to get married'. I almost wish I hadn't known. And I don't want to put it in my life story in case my parents get to know about it. Nevertheless, I feel it's part of my background so I might add that in later years.*'

On a happier note, you might get a nice surprise. Marion always felt her father didn't care very much for her because she wasn't a boy.

' *I knew he wanted a son so when I was born – the fourth of four girls – I think I was a disappointment. As I was growing up, it became a family joke that I was my parents' last-ditch attempt at having a boy. My father wasn't a man who showed his feelings much and he died five years ago. But when I was researching my life story, I spoke to his sister (my aunt). She told met that although he HAD wanted a son, he was very proud of me. She also told me a funny story about how I got my leg stuck in a chair during a Christmas lunch when I was only three. My father had to saw off part of the chair where my leg had got stuck and apparently everyone was having hysterics apart from me. My dad announced that it was a sign of character and that I clearly took after his side of the family! If I hadn't talked to my aunt, I wouldn't have known that. It made me feel a lot better about myself.* '

IF YOUR PARENTS HAVE DIED...

If you've already lost your parents, writing your life story might be particularly important to you. It's a way of filling in the pieces and leaving something to your children who don't have any grandparents to tell them tales.

So, talking to relatives or family friends about what you were like when you were little is probably one of the few 'living sources' you have at your disposal. But, just as important, they might be able to tell you what your parents were like as people. And that can also help you to understand what makes you tick.

Helen lost both her parents when she was 12 and was brought up by an aunt who lived abroad. She was sent to boarding school in England and didn't see much of the aunt except in the summer holidays. Now in her forties, she felt a need to research her life story and tracked down her mother's cousin (her first cousin once removed).

'The cousin told me that both my parents were really good at sport. My father was a keen cricketer and my mother excelled at hockey. It so happens that I was good at sport at school myself and that all three of my boys played county cricket. It was an amazing discovery and I was able to talk about it in my life story by saying that my love of sport might well have come from my parents.'

Helen's mother's cousin was also able to tell her about her parents' funeral (they had died together in a car crash).

'*Although I found it sad, it allowed me to insert details that I didn't know. For instance, no one had been able to tell me why they had chosen to be buried in a small graveyard near Plymouth. It turned out that it was because they had met nearby.*'

Not surprisingly, Helen had blocked out many of her memories around that time. But talking to the cousin, somehow released that blockage.

'*I began remembering small details such as how I would go to bed with a photograph of my parents under my pillow after the crash, in the hope it would bring them back. Although it made me feel sad to recall that, it also made me feel stronger because I can tell myself that I have survived and that I have succeeded in bringing up my own children and being there for them.*'

HOW TO FIND RELATIVES AND FRIENDS TO TALK TO

This isn't always easy. And even if you have a small core of relatives and friends who knew you as a child, it can be illuminating to spread the net and talk to others who might have different views. Try:

◆ asking your parents who their close friends were when you were born; if your parents are dead, ask relatives if they knew who your parents' friends were;

◆ looking through your parents' old address books;

- tracking down old friends/relatives of yours who knew you as a child, through Facebook or Friends Reunited or other social networking sites;
- phoning the local radio of the place where you grew up. Explain you are writing your life story and ask if they could put out an announcement saying you are keen to find someone who knew you at the time;
- putting a notice in the local paper asking for help.

Karen, who is in her early fifties, discovered her mother's best friend from going through her mother's old address book, which she had kept after her mother died five years ago.

'*I was amazed that mum's friend Sylvie was still at the same address – and still alive, as she was in her late eighties. But she told me all kinds of funny stories about myself, including the time when I was the little bridesmaid at Sylvie's wedding. My mother had apparently thought I was too young to be bridesmaid but Sylvie had insisted because I was "so sweet". But my mother was proved right because I refused to walk down the aisle after the bride. Everyone laughed and, in the end, my mother had to carry me up behind her friend. It's a story I wouldn't have known if I hadn't found Sylvie. She and Mum had lost touch after Sylvie had moved north but she was also able to tell me things about my parents. The thing that stuck in my mind was that my parents had always wanted another child but that my mum had had lots of miscarriages after me. In one way that was sad but in another, it explained why I didn't have any brothers or sisters. My parents always used to say I was very special but they were private people and never discussed why they hadn't had more children. I'm glad that I know now.*'

SUMMARY

This chapter has shown you how to do your 'verbal research'. It's hopefully given you ideas on how to talk to people (and find them) in order to find out more about yourself as you grew up and also your immediate family to put your life story into context.

Here's a quick re-cap.

- Have a good supply of pens and paper to write down your interviews. You might think you can remember conversations but it's surprising how small details get lost – and these are the details that make a story come to life.
- Ask your interviewee if you can record the conversation.
- Have a list of questions to ask relatives and friends – but be prepared to adapt your questions to follow up new leads from the answers.
- Ask relatives and friends for dates (if they can remember them) to fit the events.
- Find friends and relatives through:
  - old address books;
  - other friends and relatives;
  - Facebook;
  - Friends Reunited;
  - old school magazines.
- Write everything down in your Research Book but be prepared to leave out certain facts when you come to write the life story. You might not need it all – and you might not want to include some things.
- Use this experience as a way of getting to know yourself, and maybe your own family better.
- Don't worry about actually **writing** your life story yet – we're still doing the research bit!

Researching written records 4

Talking to relatives and friends – as described in Chapter 3 – is a great way to do research, especially as you might trigger more memories from someone just by talking to them.

But you could also add a lot more to your life story by taking the time to investigate written sources such as: formal records (your birth certificate); old letters; school reports and much more. Here's how to do it!

TRACING YOUR ANCESTORS

Most people who will read your life story will want to know how you 'sit' in the rest of your family. They'll be interested in knowing who your parents were; what they did; whether you were close to them. And they'll want to know about brothers and sisters and your own children if you have them.

It has to be said that this sort of information is probably much more interesting to people who are related to you. They are the ones who will want to know about your grandmother and the time you stayed in a wet, windy cottage in Wales with her when you were ten.

But they will also be interested in knowing about relatives who go much further back. This isn't a book on how to trace your family tree: whole tomes have been written about that and it's a lengthy exercise which can take years. But it is worth finding out about previous generations. You can start by looking up birth certificates, for example. Copies can be obtained through the General Register Office **www.direct gov.uk/gro**.

There are also several genealogical websites such as:

- **www.genesreunited.co.uk**
- **www.ancestry.co.uk**
- **www.findmypast.co.uk**
- **www.bbc.co.uk/familyhistory**

If you don't want to go to the effort of this research (and it can be very time consuming), simply find your own birth certificate or get a copy of it through the General Register Office (see above).

You can then quote from it in your life story. For instance, you could say that on your birth certificate, it shows that X was your father and that Y was your mother and that you were born in, etc.

It wouldn't be too difficult to sketch out a simple family tree – even if you limit it to one or two generations. Try to include details such as year of birth and also what people did as an occupation next to their name. It all helps to put it into context.

For example, I know that my great-great-great-grandfather Mark Lemon Romer was the first editor of *Punch* and that another great-great-grandfather John Hanson Walker was a portrait painter whose patron was Lord Frederick Leighton. But on my family tree (which my stepfather etched out as a present many years ago) there is also an intriguing name which has the word 'Disinherited' next to it. It turned out that this particular member of the family ran off with a Romany gypsy. How exciting!

As I said, the purpose of this book is not to help you write a family tree but it does help to put your own existence into its place, don't you think?

TIP   Take a photocopy of your birth certificate and stick it into your life story.

NOT FORGETTING THESE WRITTEN SO

Letters

There are also several other written s/
story. Are there any letters you can find ﹍
relatives or friends when you were younger? Or a﹍
interesting letters that they wrote to you?

Previous generations wrote letters far more than today's do, so you might well find a stash of correspondence that someone has hung on to. Ask different members of your family or have a look in old things you may have kept over the years. I don't know about you but I try to keep a certain amount of photographs (more of which later) and items (especially from when my children were young), as well as letters in old suitcases and boxes under my bed.

Gwen, one of my students who is now in her late forties, found some letters to her mother from her grandmother. She used the following paragraph in her life story.

' *When my mother went into a home recently, I had to sort out her personal possessions and found a letter from her aunt (my great-aunt). It started like this. "Darling Julia, I'm so thrilled that you finally had your much longed-for baby daughter after three boys! I do understand how much you wanted a girl. Sadly, as you know, I never had that gift myself but I am over the moon that you will be able to have that wonderful mother/daughter relationship that your own mother and I had with our mother. Well done! What a clever girl you are!"* '

Gwen was really touched to find the letter, especially as her great-aunt was no longer alive.

' *It made me feel closer to her and also told me something I didn't know. I'd never really thought much about being the youngest of four although I did like having older brothers. But my aunt's letter made me feel rather special.* '

Baby books

Just as previous generations tended to write more letters, so they also kept Baby Books; a written record of baby's development. Perhaps your parents did the same. If so, do they still have them or was it passed down to you? Maybe it's in that old suitcase of 'rubbish' in the attic! It's definitely worth sifting through to see if you can come up with anything.

Birth announcements

Do you have any old newspaper clippings with a birth announcement in it? If not, is it possible that your parents might have put an announcement in the local paper or a national paper? It's worth contacting the archives department of, say, a national newspaper and a local one to find out. If so, you could mention it in your life story and also use it as a visual decoration by sticking it in.

Christening gifts

Have you kept any of your christening gifts? Most of us have the odd silver spoon or mug that we were given at our christening. If so, is there a little note inside the box from the sender? Marian, another student, who decided to write her life story when she got to 65, was thrilled to find a small note in a box containing a set of silver spoons which she had been given by a grandfather.

' *It asked my mother to give me the spoons when I had a home of my own. In fact, she didn't – she must have forgotten – and it only came to me when my sister found them in a suitcase of old things that she was going through. The letter was on headed notepaper which made it even more precious because I could remember the house. We used to visit it regularly as children. Now I use the spoons on special occasions and I have also mentioned them in my life story.* '

Old books

If, like me, you love browsing through second-hand bookshops, you'll probably stop to think sometimes when you come across an inscription. Here's one I found recently:

'To Cyril on his twenty-first birthday, October 1932.'

It was written in lovely copperplate writing and I can't help wondering what happened to Cyril and why he didn't keep the book or whether someone saw fit to get rid of it when he died.

You could also go through old books that you had as a child and see if it leads to inspiration. Caroline, for example, now in her fifties, has kept some of her children's books. When writing her life story, she rang me excitedly to say she had found an inscription in one from her mother. *'To Caroline, for being such a good girl.'*

'I can actually remember when she gave it to me. It was when my baby brother was born – and it brought back all kinds of memories. It also helped me list the kind of children's books I enjoyed when I was a child and I put this list into my life story. For instance, I loved Brer Rabbit *and, when I was older,* Swallows and Amazons *by Arthur Ransome.'*

Old birthday and Christmas cards
If you're a hoarder, you may well have kept some of these. (I personally tend to keep special cards inside books for a future generation to discover!) Go through family 'rubbish' and see if you can find some yourself. Again, the writing and names might help you think of previous memories.

Old comics/newspapers
Unless you're a real hoarder (or your parents were) you probably haven't got any newspapers or magazines or comics from your childhood. But it is still possible to obtain copies from dealers or the internet. Examples of websites dealing in this include **www.yeoldcomicbookstore.com** and also **www.loot.com/advert/old-comics**.

You might like to get one from the year of your birth or perhaps a copy of a comic that you used to read as a child. There are collectors of comics like *Eagle* and *June & Schoolfriend*. Again, you could stick them in your life story as illustrations.

You could also use the newspapers to record global world events that happened around your birth or during your childhood. For instance, Eric, another life story student, has collected articles about the Cuban crisis in the 1960s from old newspapers and stuck those in his life story.

Medical record cards

Don't dismiss anything in your search for source material for your life story! Parents tended to be very organised in the past so you might find a copy of your medical card or even your birth tag like Christine did.

' *I was sorting through some old pictures and bits and pieces the other day, and came across a small tag that gave my maiden name. It's also got the date of my birth and even the time so I've stuck that into my life story.* '

School reports

These can be a fantastic source for finding out what you were like as a child. They can also bring a lot of humour. Ask relatives if they have copies or maybe contact your old school to see if they have some documents about you. Perhaps there is a school prospectus which you can use.

Here's one which one of my life story students found.

' *Peter is not as conscientious as I would have liked. His attention keeps wandering, especially if there is Games in the afternoon. He needs to work harder at logarithms.* '

This caused quite a lot of laughs in Peter's family when they read this as Peter then went onto become a financial adviser after university! Peter also used his old school report as an illustration by sticking it onto the typed pages of his life story.

School books

Are there any old school books of yours that your mother has kept with your childish writing? If so, you could use them to trigger old memories. Anne discovered an old history book which helped her to remember a teacher whom she hadn't thought about for years.

‘*She was very strict but when she got onto the Tudors her whole face came alive and she filled us with enthusiasm.*’

Anne was then able to write about the teacher and also used the page as an illustration in her life story.

HOW TO USE THIS MATERIAL

With any luck, you'll have built up quite a collection of papers by now. I suggest buying a document folder with different sections and organising your papers. Label one section 'Letters' and another 'Cards', etc.

All this, together with the results of your efforts from previous chapters, is a crucial part of your research. We are now ready to use this to start writing your life story!

SUMMARY

- ◆ Don't dismiss any kind of written record of your life. It could be just what you need to shed some light on your 'early' days. Look out for:
  - birth certificate;
  - old birthday cards (and Christmas, etc.);
  - medical records;
  - school books;
  - school reports;
  - letters.
- ◆ Also try to sketch out a family tree. It doesn't matter if you can only go back for a couple of generations. Even the mention of a grandparent or great-grandparent will help future readers to put your own life into context.
- ◆ Buy a folder with various compartments and use it to store your research findings.

Step Four

Different Ways of Structuring Your Life Story

How to structure your life story: chronologically 5

The good news is that you've done a lot of the hard work already. In this section (Chapters 5–11) I'm going to suggest different ways of structuring and writing your life story from the research that you have done. It's up to you to choose the one that appeals to you most but it's also worth experimenting with different formats. You might be pleasantly surprised.

However, whichever format you choose, it's vital that you think about your writing patterns before you begin. Do you want to write your life story by hand? The advantage of this is that it will have a very personal flavour with your handwriting. On the other hand, will everyone be able to read it? Can you afford to pay for someone to type it up? Or can you type it yourself? The advantage of this is that you can add lines easily on a computer when you want to change something. And it will probably be easier for others to read.

This is something that you can best decide for yourself. But if you do choose to write it by hand, I would suggest finding a nicely bound book with lines from a good stationer. And, if you type it, please back up your work by transferring it regularly to a memory stick or sending it as an attachment to yourself so you can access it, if necessary, from someone else's computer. There'll be more advice on this in Chapter 21 on Presentation.

USING THE SIMPLE CHRONOLOGICAL APPROACH

This involves looking at your life in blocks. In other words, dividing it into sections such as The Early Years (birth to five years); Early Childhood (five to twelve); The Teenage Years (thirteen to nineteen); Young Adult (twenty to thirty-five or thereabouts); Middle Years (thirty-five to about fifty); and Later Years (fifty upwards).

The simple act of breaking down your life into manageable bits makes the task far less daunting. Of course, you will be able to write about some sections far more easily than others. You'll remember things that have happened to you more easily than those that took place years ago.

Or will you? This is where your research will be so handy. Let's take The Early Years. You've already got – perhaps – a birth certificate, so you can tell the reader where you were born and who your parents were.

You've also got a piece of paper where you wrote down what your first memory was – or, as we've said, an early memory, since it's difficult to know what is actually a very first one.

You may have cards that were sent to your parents when you were born. Or photographs that showed your parents holding you that you can use to illustrate this section. You have? Great. Then let's get going.

HOW TO START

Even though you may already have written an introduction (see Chapter 1), I would still suggest beginning with an opening paragraph that tells the reader when you were born and gives a brief outline of your background. Give it a title at the top; for example 'An Introduction to Myself'. Here is an example from one of my students, Eleanor, who has kindly agreed to give an illustration.

‘ *I was born in 1934, a few years before the start of the Second World War. My parents had only got married the year before so I was their first child. They lived just outside Newcastle where my father worked as a shopkeeper in his father's grocery business.* ’

THE EARLY YEARS

Then I would head the next section 'The Early Years' and begin with a description of your first memory. If you can, say how old you were when you think this happened and give as much detail as possible. Below is an example from Eleanor's life again.

'*One of my first memories is helping my father in the shop. I was allowed to help put out crates of fruit in front of the shop. I remember they were heavy to move but I felt very grown up, being allowed to help. As a treat, I was sometimes given an orange!*'

After that, still in the second section, I suggest a short description of anything else you remember between the ages of babyhood and five. Try to write this as though you were chatting to a friend. A life story doesn't have to be written like a text book with long, formal words. In fact, it's much more readable if it sounds like a conversation.

Here is Eleanor again:

'*I remember that when the Second World War broke out, the boy next door went away to join up. His mother came round to tell my mother and we all sat round the kitchen table, listening to the radio. I didn't realise how serious things were: in fact, I clearly remember playing a soldier game outside in the yard with the children on the other side of the house. I also remember that there wasn't much fruit any more in the shop because of the war.*'

If you're stuck on what to write, try to think about the following subjects, which might trigger off a memory.

♦ Going to school.
♦ The birth of a brother or sister.
♦ A favourite toy.
♦ A world event that shaped your life.
♦ Something that frightened you or made you happy.

GETTING BIGGER

You see – you've written quite a bit already! Now it's time to remember what you can remember about the years from five to twelve. The good thing about this section is that it covers a big developmental phase in most people's lives. So although you might not remember much about when you were five, you probably do remember quite a lot about when you were ten.

Here are some triggers to help.

- Friends at school.
- Hobbies, e.g. riding; stamp collecting; playing the piano.
- Visiting relatives.
- Pets.
- School uniform.

Here is a memory from Sally. It's worth saying that several people's life stories feature the Second World War because it was an important part of many older people's lives and still is today. Even if you weren't born when the war ended, it is bound to have affected your immediate family.

'*I was eight when the Second World War started and I remember when the doodle bug bombs started to fall. My mother had taught me to listen for that whining noise and had said that when the noise stopped, that was the dangerous time because then the bomb was about to fall. One day, I was walking to school with my younger brother when I heard that whining noise. Luckily we were near a disused bridge so I pushed my little brother underneath and then rushed in after him. Seconds later, there was a terrible noise. The bomb had fallen on the path we had just been on. Luckily we weren't hurt and although the bridge shook, it stayed intact and protected us. Amazingly, we carried on walking to school!*'

THE TEENAGE YEARS

This section generally gets easier. Most of us can remember certain stages in our teenage lives; in fact, many of us would prefer to forget them.

You might get inspiration from the following:

- first boyfriend/girlfriend;
- exams;
- rows with parents;
- clothes;
- films we saw;
- dances;
- holidays.

DAVID'S MEMORIES

'*I remember being at boarding school during the late 1960s when there were some important exams going on. We spent a lot of time listening to music on our transistor radios in the dorm. Then one day, someone wished me good luck for an exam later that day and I thought "What is he talking about? The exam isn't until next week." But then I found out that my friend was right and that there WAS an exam! I didn't do very well but it taught me to be prepared in the future!*'

MARILYN

'*I remember being allowed to stay up late and watch the landing of the first man on the moon. I was 11 at the time and it seemed incredible that someone could actually go so far. My mum, dad and my sister all crowded round our black and white television set but all I could remember were a few blurred white shapes and the excitement that I'd been allowed up so late!*'

YOUNG ADULT

You see! It's getting easier and easier. Now I want you to try and include as many emotions as you can, as well as the factual bits. You may well have been able to do this in the previous section when you talked about being a teenager. Most of us remember how our hearts were broken or how we broke someone else's heart.

Try thinking about the following:

- first job;
- meeting your husband/wife;
- special friends;
- money;
- moving house;
- having children.

' *I remember when we were first married, Maggie Thatcher was made prime minister. It seemed incredible that we had a woman in charge of the country! My husband and I had just bought our first flat. It was in a grotty part of London but we loved it! Every now and then the lights would go out because we kept forgetting to save change for the meter. On Saturdays, we would get our vegetables from the market and I felt very grown up. I was only 21 when I got married but it didn't seem young in those days. Neither of us could drive a car because lessons were expensive so we got the 38 bus instead into the centre of London to go to work. We didn't have much money but we were very happy.*'

MIDDLE YEARS

Some of the subjects we've just covered might not crop up until this section, depending on how your life pattern has been. Meanwhile, here are some other subjects that you might want to write about.

- How you enjoyed yourself.
- Bereavements – losing someone important.
- Changing jobs/houses.
- Changes of direction.
- New marriage.

GEOFFREY'S STORY

' *When I was nearly 40, my boss called me into the office one day and asked if I wanted to manage a new banking branch near Winchester. My wife and I had lived in Manchester all our lives and we'd never even been to Winchester before. But we both felt it might be an adventure. Our two boys didn't really want to leave their friends but we liked the look of the schools in the new area so tried to persuade them they would be happy. In fact, it was a good decision although I'm glad we didn't know what was going to happen next...*

This is getting more interesting, isn't it? By creating tension like this, Geoffrey is making us read on.

Within three years, I was called into head office again and told that the branch was closing. I was given a choice; either I could go back to Manchester or take the pay package they were offering. I chose the latter and decided to use it to set up a decorating business. It was completely different from banking but by then, that's exactly what I needed. By then, the boys were old enough to join and they still run the firm, even though I've retired.

LATER YEARS

There's no excuse for not being able to think of something to write for this section – unless you have a severe memory loss. But if you do need triggers, here are some things to think about.

- Jobs.
- Money.
- Family.
- Triumphs.
- Tragedies.
- Joys.
- Fears.
- Grandchildren?
- Weddings.

SANDRA (49)

Five years ago, I bought a lottery ticket on impulse and didn't bother checking it until the following Wednesday. To my amazement, I discovered I had four matching numbers! I thought there was a mistake and didn't even tell my husband until I had rung up Camelot. My heart was beating with a mixture of excitement and disbelief. Part of me had always dreamed of a windfall but part of me didn't want to have a lot of money – I'd read too many stories about people's lives being ruined by a big win. Then the girl at the other end said I had won just over £2000. I was thrilled! My husband and I spent it on a Caribbean cruise; something we'd always wanted to do. '

NOTE: Sandra went on to write a daily diary of her three-week cruise, which she then attached to her life story as an extra at the end.

Conclusion of your life story

I'm going to show you how to end your life story in Chapter 18 – and trust me, it doesn't have to be morbid! In fact, it can be very upbeat and some students have found it of great inspiration. So trust me on this!

Summary

One method of structuring your life story is to tell it in chronological order. The advantages of this is that you don't need to remember every year of your life! You can do it by thinking of as many incidents and stories as possible from different sections of your life such as:

- Introduction; brief description of your background, including when you were born;
- The Early Years (birth to five);
- Early Childhood (five to twelve);
- The Teenage Years (thirteen to nineteen);
- Young Adults (twenty to thirty-five);
- The Middle Years (thirty-five to fifty-ish);
- Later Years (fifty upwards).

It doesn't matter if you can only remember one or two incidents from each chunk. The chances are that once you have started, you will begin to recall more. And then you can go back and add to it.

Verdict
Arthur (65)
' This was a straightforward method which appealed to me because I've got a good memory. I can remember things that happened several years ago, clearer than something that

happened last week. It did take time – I worked on my life story for a couple of hours every week and completed it after ten months. But I feel it produced a piece of writing which I'm proud of and which will last for several generations with any luck. It was also a good retirement project for me!'

6 *How to structure your life story by using specific timespans*

If you are a very methodical person or have a particularly good memory, you might be able to write your life story by dividing it into more specific dates. For example, depending on your age, you might write your memories under the following headings: 1945–1955; 1955–1965 and so on.

It's quite a good idea to keep the different chunks of years in the same equal weightings. For example, chunks of ten years as I have shown above or maybe chunks of fifteen years such as 1945–1960.

Do bear in mind that if you have large life chunks of over ten years, you could find yourself lumping several important bits together without doing them individual justice. I personally feel that ten-year gaps are pretty 'achievable' and that you can generally include useful memories and events. You might even be able to do this with five-year gaps, although that depends on your memory and also how eventful your life has been!

ADVANTAGES OF THIS METHOD

It's easier for you to think of events from long ago if we are looking at ten-year chunks. Most of us, if pushed, will think of something important to us that happened before the age of ten, for instance. It might be a new school. Or moving house. Or a new brother or sister.

Similarly, if we had to think of something momentous that occurred in our teenage years, most of us would come up with something. It could be a first love or it might be a first job or it could be taking an important exam.

You can also have a smaller section at the end of those ten years when you can list other things that happened even if you don't recall them in as much detail as the main event.

Here's an example from Anne, one of my life story students. It's rather sad but she says it helped her release some of her feelings when she wrote about it. She used the ten-year scheme to write her life story and put this in the years 1970–1980. Because the following event was so significant, she remembered the exact date but this isn't always necessary if it's in a block of years.

‘ *I remember coming home on February 4th 1972 to find my neighbour at the front door instead of my mother. She told me that Mum had had to go out somewhere and had asked her to be there to cook me supper and keep an eye on my younger brother who was watching television in our sitting room.*

We had fish fingers and chips on my mum's best china plates with brown and cream edges round them – I remember that clearly although later, I couldn't understand why I remembered small details like that. And afterwards, I helped her wash up before I sat down at the kitchen table to do my long division. Again, I remember the details quite clearly. By then, it was getting dark and I kept asking where Mum was. Then the neighbour, who was a nice woman without children of her own, said I had to be very brave. She sat me down, took my hands in hers and said my father had been knocked off his bike and was very ill. My mother was with him at the hospital.

I cried a bit but then went on with my homework. Looking back, I don't know how I could have done that and in years to come, I felt guilty at not having demanded to go and see my mother to keep her company. I was 14 at the time and surely old enough to have done that. But in our day, we did what adults said so I just waited for mum to come back.

My brother was asleep when she finally did and when she came in through the door, she had her sunglasses on which seemed strange because it was night. I asked how Dad was and she said he was fine. Then we all went to bed although in the night, I woke up to hear Mum crying. I went into her room to see if she needed anything and then she told me that Dad had died the previous day. She hadn't wanted to tell me when she'd come in because she thought I'd take the news better in the morning. I wanted to cry but the tears wouldn't come.

I never saw his body and my brother and I didn't go to Dad's funeral. We weren't asked and we didn't think of asking if we could go. Later, as an adult, I discussed it with Mum and she said she had wanted to protect me. This experience affected me for years and I'm still scared of people not telling me the truth. I have promised my own children that I will always tell them everything.'

I said it was sad, didn't I? But the good side is that, for Anne, it was a great relief to write it all down. It was also helpful for her to show her page to her husband and teenage children because she'd never been able to put her experience into words, before. Interestingly, it helped her brother too because he had been too young to have remembered much of it, apart from the obvious fact that Dad wasn't around any more.

After that, Anne then wrote down a list of events in the rest of this decade (1970–1980). She couldn't recall much detail but some of the events speak for themselves:

'*O levels. I took eight and passed seven of them with pretty high grades. Mum was so pleased that she took me to the cinema and we saw David Essex in* That'll Be The Day.

Moving house. I can't remember when exactly but we moved from London to Essex to be near my grandparents (mum's parents). I was sad to leave my friends, especially Christine from school. At first I didn't like the new one but then we did a school play and I was chosen to be a fairy in Midsummer's Night Dream. *That helped me make friends, including my best friend Helen who later became Godmother to my children.*

A levels. Although I got the grades I needed, I'd decided by then that I didn't want to go to university. So I went straight to teacher training college instead. I really loved it and decided to specialise in teaching little ones. '

DISADVANTAGES OF THIS METHOD

You might have spotted some of these already! Although Anne's story about her father's death was very powerful, it makes the other events seem a little weak. However, just by asking yourself some simple questions, you can bump up the detail and make them stronger. I asked Anne to think about the following:

Where did you take your O levels and did you work hard for them?

She came up with the following:

' *We had to take our exams in the school hall. All the usual rows of chairs were cleared away and tables and chairs were put out with our exam numbers on them. It was very scary. I did revise hard because of my father. He always encouraged me to work and I wanted to get good grades for him. We were all allowed to take a lucky memento into our exams and I took in his photograph. Looking at that during my exam, made me determined to get the best mark I could.* '

Now this has really added something to it, hasn't it?

BOOSTING YOUR OWN MEMORIES

Ask yourself:

- What, were, when, who, where and how.
- What were you doing? What were others doing? When were you doing it? Where were you doing it and what was the place like?
- Who else was there? What did they look like?
- How did you do it? Did you have anyone or anything to help?

I'LL NEVER FORGET THE DAY/WEEK/MONTH/YEAR WHEN...

Sometimes, there's one really big event that dominates your life and some students just want to write about that. It might be the Second World War. Or it could be emigrating. It might be a marriage. Or it might be a death.

The rest of your life might, in comparison, fade into insignificance or you might simply not want to write about it.

If so, there's nothing wrong with taking just one period of your life and writing about that. It won't take so much time to research; indeed, it might all be in your head right now.

Geoff, one of my life students, came to me because he wanted to write about his experiences during the war when he was shot down by the Germans over Norway. Just like my uncle, he was looked after by the locals but then gave himself up when it was made known that the locals would be shot if they were found to be harbouring the 'enemy'. He wrote about giving himself up and then spending two years in a POW camp.

' *I didn't want to write about the rest of my life. I just wanted to write this part down so my grandchildren would have it when I am gone. I have tried telling them bits of it now but they don't seem interested. My daughter persuaded me to write it as a short life story for when they ARE old enough to want to know more.* '

In fact, Geoff's grandchildren DID want to know more – including what happened when he was released. So this is what he wrote:

' *Coming back was unreal – words can't describe how it felt to see my mum and dad again. I was lucky because I then got an apprenticeship as an engineer and then got sent abroad to South Africa with my work for a few years before coming back to the UK.* '

When Geoff wrote this sentence, I pointed out that he had managed to cram rather a lot into one paragraph and that he could easily take parts out and elaborate to make a fuller story. So he then wrote about life as an apprentice in post-war Britain and then about being an ex-pat in South Africa where he met and married his wife. After that, as he wrote, the political situation made them feel uncomfortable so they came back to the UK.

If you find yourself writing a long sentence with a great deal going on in it, like Geoff, make yourself go back and write about each event in more detail. Otherwise it can be very frustrating for future readers to miss out on something that sounds interesting but which isn't covered enough!

SUMMARY

+ Try the ten- or five-year chunk method.
+ Advantages: you only need to think of one or two big events for each section. You can then list the others.
+ Disadvantages: it might not give others such a wide overall view of your life as a complete life story would.
+ BUT you can ask yourself questions about minor events to create more details.
+ It can also be a good method for students who want to concentrate only on a particularly significant part of their life.
+ Beware of 'throwing away' good stories by dismissing them in a few lines. Milk their potential by including how you felt and what the place/situation was like.

Verdict
EILEEN (78)

'*I'm quite a methodical person so I liked this method. Because I'm no spring chicken, it would have been a big project to have written about every single year of my life. Instead, I did it in ten-year chunks which allowed me to "cherry pick" certain events in my life and skate over the ones I didn't want to remember!*'

7 *Where were you when...?*

Here's another way to write your life story. I think it's a really gripping method – and one which everyone will want to read. I call it the 'Where were you when...?' method.

Start off by jotting down a list of worldwide events that most people will remember and then recalling where you were at that particular time. For instance, when President Kennedy was shot, I can remember getting ready for bed and then coming down to kiss my parents goodnight as a child. I must have heard that the president had been shot on the radio or television or maybe through my parents, because I can recall asking my father if the president had died. I can still remember his words. 'I'm afraid that he has.'

An anecdote like that might not have seemed very significant at the time or maybe even now. But in years to come, it might seem like a slice of history to a future grandchild, say, living in the middle of the 21st century.

I could embellish it by talking about the fact that at that time – I was about eight – I shared a bedroom with my sister and we lived in a suburb in North London. I might also talk about the school I went to and what I enjoyed doing. In this way, I would be telling my own life story but using a world event – the death of Kennedy – as a trigger.

Below are some examples of some worldwide events and some quotes from students who have used this to write a bit about their own life story.

THE DEATH OF DIANA, PRINCESS OF WALES, 1997

' *I had just had the worst week of my life – my husband had told me he was in love with someone else and wanted to leave. I asked him to stay and he said he'd tell me in the morning if he would or not. I can honestly say that I didn't have a wink of sleep all night. When we woke up, I turned on the radio because I was too scared to ask if he would stay or not. I wanted things to be normal again. I heard the broadcaster talking about Diana and her campaign to get rid of landmines and I thought "Surely she hasn't been blown up?"*

I ran downstairs and turned on the television. To my horror, there were pictures everywhere of Diana. I thought "She can't possibly be dead. What has happened?" And then the reporter brought everyone up to date by talking about the crash. I ran back upstairs and woke up my husband. "Diana's dead," I said.

There was a pause. "All right, I'll stay," he said.

I know it's awful but I was almost grateful to Diana. If it hadn't been the shock of her death and the thought of that family being broken up again, I think my husband might have gone. But he could see how much we all had to lose if he went. Ironically, our marriage did break up two years later but Diana gave us that extra time. '

This was written by Mandy, a life story student. She then went on to talk about how she coped with life as a single mother. Happily, it wasn't all doom and gloom.

' *I somehow managed to get a job at a local department store. All my qualifications were out of date so I couldn't find anything else but actually, I loved it! After being a full time mum for years, I enjoyed being with others and found that there were lots of people in the same position as me. Two of them suggested I went Salsa dancing with them on Friday night and so I did while a friend babysat for the boys.* '

Later in Mandy's life story, she describes how she met her future husband.

'I'd been promoted then at the store and Geoff joined the menswear department. He had never been married – in fact he was younger than me so I didn't see him as a possible boyfriend. I think that's why it worked because we were so natural with each other. When he first asked me out, I was surprised but went because he'd suggested seeing a film we both wanted to see. At the end, he kissed me and it felt as though a thunder bolt went through me. We both looked at each other in surprise and we haven't been apart since!'

By the time you get to this point, you almost forget that Mandy's life story was inspired by her memory of Diana's death. But at the same time, the latter provides a good starting point and one which has a historical significance for all readers both present and future.

Here are some more life stories and their links to historical events:

9/11

HEATHER
'We had just moved to New York because of my husband's job and I heard the news through a neighbour. Luckily, my husband had been out of the city that day for a meeting but otherwise, he would have been in one of the twin towers. The experience really shook us both and made us realise how lucky we were. It was a very dramatic introduction to living abroad.'

Heather used this experience to kick-start her life story about living in New York. She wanted to write it as a memoir so she would remember, in years to come, the sort of small details that we forget during a big adventure.

THE QUEEN'S CORONATION 1953

LILIAN

' *I'm the same age as the Queen so, like many young girls of the time, I took a keen interest in both her wedding and her coronation. We all thought she was wonderful. I was in the crowd cheering her on outside Westminster Abbey; in fact, I met my future husband Stan in the crowd. He lifted me up so I could see what was going on!*

Stan and I got married the following year and I gave up work (as a seamstress) which often happened in those days. Husbands didn't always like their wives to work because it suggested they couldn't provide for them themselves! Unlike the Queen, our new home was much smaller. In fact, we started off with Stan's parents which again, was quite common. It took us another five years until we could afford a place of our own and by then, we had two little girls. '

Lilian went on to write her life story, using the coronation as a starting point. She described her married life with Stan, which was happy, but had its occasional ups and downs. She also talked about holidays on the south coast and her excitement at getting a new washing machine. It's not a life story which is packed with earth-moving events but it provides a gentle look at the 1950s through to the present day. Lilian wanted to write her life story for her grandchildren because they had asked her for some of her memories for a school project. 'That inspired me to write more and to my surprise, my granddaughters were really interested.'

7/7

JULIA

' *I was on my way to a job interview and almost got one of the tubes that was blown up. When I missed it, I was really upset because I thought I was going to be late. So I decided to walk instead. When I reached the firm where I was having the interview, everyone was talking about the news. Some of the girls were late, apparently, and people were worried that they'd been caught up in it. (As I later found out, they hadn't.)*

I got the job partly because the news shook me up so much that I forgot to be frightened; usually in job interviews, I seize up with nerves. But it really made me think about life.

In fact, because of 7/7, I turned down the job offer and moved out to the country instead. It wasn't that I was scared of travelling in London; it was just that I'd always meant to move out one day and almost being caught up in a tragedy like that, made me realise that you should live for the moment.

Julia then went on to write about her new life, helping to run a livery stables in Somerset. But the 7/7 tragedy provided a good starting point.

Here are some other worldwide events that might provide inspiration for your life story:

♦ the three-day week;
♦ Concorde's first flight;
♦ Margaret Thatcher's election as prime minister;
♦ the start of Freddie Laker package holidays;
♦ the knocking down of the Berlin Wall;
♦ the death of Sir Winston Churchill;
♦ England winning the World Cup in 1966;
♦ the Cuban Missile Crisis;
♦ the 2004 tsunami.

Summary

♦ Linking your own life story with a big national event gives an extra significance to your tale. It sets your story in a historical context and makes it more interesting to readers.
♦ You can start by remembering where you were when this event happened and then use it to kick-start a story about your own life.

Verdict
Pamela (69)

The downside was that I had to do more research than I realised to check up on historical details like facts and make sure they were accurate. I mentioned the Cuban Missile Crisis for instance and had to check when it actually happened. But the plus was that it put my life story into a historical context and everyone who reads it can relate to it because they then tell me what was happening in their lives at that time.'

8 *Desert Island Discs method*

If you listen to *Desert Island Discs* on Radio 4 (currently aired on Fridays and Sundays), you'll know that it comprises an interview with a celebrity who recalls different stages of their life in chunks. At the end of each short chunk, the celebrity thinks of a favourite piece of music which reminds them of that time or which has some sort of significance for them.

This is a great way for anyone to tell their life story on paper! And you don't have to be famous to do it.

How to start...

Write down five important things that have happened to you in your life. Try to spread them out so you have about one or two things in each five- or ten-year chunks of your life between the ages of birth and now.

For example, you might begin by thinking of your life up to the age of ten or maybe fifteen, depending on how old you are. Begin by writing down a few lines about your background. Include the following topics.

- ◆ Where you were brought up.
- ◆ What your parents did (if you lived with your parents).
- ◆ Family (brothers, aunts, etc.).
- ◆ What you liked doing at school.

Here's an example from Samantha, 54, one of my life story students.

'*I was born in 1955 and was brought up in Cardiff along with my two sisters. My dad worked for the local newspaper and my mum, who used to be a nurse, stayed at home to look after us which was the norm in those days. We had lots of family nearby including several aunts and cousins. On Sundays, we'd usually go round to each other's homes for tea which was good fun. I remember my dad getting a car when I was young (possibly about four although I'm not certain) and we used to go out for day trips to places like Penarth.*

I went to the local school where I was quite happy. My favourite subject was Nature and I still have an exercise book with drawings of wild flowers!

PIECE OF MUSIC

'My parents had a gramophone in the living room. It was like a big box with some shiny LPs stacked next to it. I knew them all off by heart. They were a mixture of pop songs like Helen Shapiro and also classical music such as Fingal's Cave. I also had some of my own records although they were small; we called them 45s. The one I remember best was about a toy character called Twizzle! I think there was music on it but I'm not sure so I'm going to choose Fingal's Cave for my first piece of music.'

Then go on to another stage of your life – say between ten and twenty. Write down anything you can remember about:

♦ school;
♦ college (if applicable);
♦ your first job;
♦ falling in love.

'I worked hard at school and although I wasn't naturally bright, I got reasonable A level grades and went on to read Geography.'

I'm afraid that I stopped Samantha here and encouraged her to go back and fill in the gaps in this sentence because I felt she had jumped too far! So this is her re-draft:

'I found it hard to keep up at school unless I worked hard. So every evening, I would go up to my bedroom and do my homework. To be honest, I also liked being away from my family! I wasn't a rebellious teenager but I did like having time to myself. However, I had a great friend called Christine who lived round the corner and we would often go to school discos together. They were very tame affairs compared with clubs nowadays. We'd all dance around our handbags unless it was a "slow dance" when it was permitted for boys to hold us. That's how I met my first boyfriend Chris! He was at the boys' school and we went out for nearly a year when I was 17. In those days, it wasn't done to go too far, as it was called, so our relationship was quite innocent! I was really upset when he and his family then moved away. I still wonder what happened to him.'

Now THIS is more interesting, isn't it?

Samantha's music for this period.

'It has to be "Bridge Over Troubled Water" by Simon and Garfunkle. Chris and I used to listen to it for hours and it still makes me feel weak at the knees to hear it!'

Stage Three of your Desert Island Discs method might take in the next ten years and so on.

At the end of every section, think of a song or piece of music without words that reminds you of that time and say why. Try to keep each of your five sections quite short; anything from one page to about five.

ADVANTAGE OF THE DESERT ISLAND DISCS FORMAT

It doesn't take long to complete and it's fun to write! Readers will be interested in your choice of music.

DISADVANTAGES OF THE DESERT ISLAND DISCS FORMAT

The short length will mean that you probably miss things out.

At the end of the *Desert Island Discs* programme on the radio, participants are asked to name a luxury and also a favourite book that they would take onto an island if they were deserted. You could do the same and then explain why it means a lot to you. Again, this will tell readers more about your life.

SAMANTHA'S FAVOURITE BOOK

'Jane Eyre. *I read it first at school but then read it again recently when one of my daughters had it as a school text. The characters are so enthralling that I would read it again and again.*'

SAMANTHA'S LUXURY

' *It would have to be one of those deep, stand alone baths with an unending supply of hot water, luxury soap and big white fluffy towels! As my husband and girls will tell you, I spend ages in the bathroom at night!*'

SUMMARY

The Desert Island Discs method is a fun way of telling your own life.

♦ It won't take long and the music, luxury and chosen book all add different dimensions.

Verdict

IAN (43)

'I liked this way of writing my life story. It wasn't as difficult as I thought and I had a lot of fun thinking about the songs I chose. It didn't take too long to write and yet it still gave a balanced picture of my life.'

9 *You've got a first!*

This is a really whacky way of writing your life story. It's fun to write and fun to read. No one can resist reading a line that starts 'My first boyfriend was called Bob' or 'My first kiss took place in the local village hall'!

The joy of this method is that it is made up of lots of short, snappy anecdotes which you will have fun remembering. Honestly!

HOW TO START

Think about the following headings and put a tick by the ones that you can remember. You might not be sure if your memory is of the very first time that you did something but that doesn't matter. The important thing is that it's the first time YOU remember.

- First school.
- First time that you rode a bike.
- First time that you went on holiday (or remember going on holiday).
- First time that you moved house.
- First time that you went to the cinema or theatre.
- First time that you achieved something important.
- First time that you went to Brownies or Cubs.
- First time that you went away without your parents.
- First time that you took an exam.
- First girlfriend/boyfriend.
- First kiss.
- First dance.
- First special outfit.
- First trip abroad.
- First time on a plane/boat/water-skis, etc.
- First experience of death.

- First job.
- First house of your own.
- First marriage.
- First child.

And so on! We could go on for ages.

Now, go back over the subjects you've put a tick next to. What can you remember, for instance, about your first school?

MY FIRST...

Here's what Jill, one of my students, wrote:

MY FIRST SCHOOL

❛*When I was about five, my parents sent me to a small school in the Surrey village where we lived. We wore a green uniform (funnily enough I haven't been able to wear green since!) and I remember sitting at a wooden desk with an inkwell in it. We wrote with proper fountain pens and sometimes I would come back with ink splashes on my sleeve which my mother wasn't very pleased about! My favourite subject was geography because I liked the teacher. She was very jolly although I can't remember her name. I was fascinated by the big pink and green map on the wall of the classroom and wanted to know how I could get to all those places. Later in life, I travelled for two years so I often think that my wanderlust began at my first school!*

At break time, we used to play skipping rope games. We'd have to run from one side to the other and duck under the rope so it didn't hit us. We also played tennis against the wall at the back. In summer, we would sit in the playground where there was a patch of grass and make daisy and buttercup chains.❜

There's nothing awe-inspiring here, granted, but it's a nice picture of a school in the 1950s, isn't it? Jill's grandchildren were fascinated by the idea of inkwells and wanted to know why their grandmother didn't have a computer!

This memory comes from Mary, a life story student.

FIRST TIME THAT WE MOVED HOUSE

'*During the 1950s and early 1960s, my parents and I used to live with my grandmother and I didn't realise that was unusual until I was older. Then, when I was about 12, my mother said we were going to have our own house. I didn't want to leave my grandmother but I was also excited because my parents said I'd be able to have a room of my own.*

I remember my grandmother being upset because we were going. Later I found out that my mother had been desperate to have her own place instead of sharing with her mother-in-law. I can't remember the packing although I do recall being told to go back to the new house after school that day (it was only round the corner from the old one). It seemed very exciting to go through a new front door and discovering my mother and all our old things in a new place! I also remember the smell of new carpets and my mother's excited smile. Even better, there was a little gate at the end of the garden which led into a lane where my friend Lucy lived. So it was easy to go out and see her! We were also still near by my grandmother so I would go and see her every day. She took in a lodger after we left which seemed rather strange. I think I was a bit jealous of her because my grandmother enjoyed her company too.'

There's a lot in this, isn't there? We can sense a fairly troubled emotional background to Mary's past and indeed, this is one reason why she wanted to write her life story. Her mother hadn't enjoyed living with her mother-in-law and this had a knock-on effect on her parents' marriage. Writing about her life story using the First method, however, made it easier for Mary. This is what she wrote on a slightly lighter subject!

MY FIRST KISS!

'*My first kiss happened during the first dance I ever went to with my friend Lucy. Twice a year, her school was invited to the local boys' school dance and she always managed to wangle me an invitation (my school didn't believe in dances!). My mother made me a dress out of shiny blue and pink material which I loved! In those days, mothers often made clothes for their children out of dress patterns that came with magazines.*

The dance was held in a hall and there were lots of bright white lights that lit up your clothes! I felt very shy dancing around on my own because my friend Lucy was asked to dance right at the beginning. Then a boy came towards me and asked me, with a nice smile, if I would like to dance. I felt both relieved and excited and afraid at the same time! His name was Chris and he was doing his A levels at school (he was 17 and I was 16). We had four or five dances and then he bought me a soft drink. Then the DJ announced it was going to be a slow dance and my heart fluttered. It seemed very strange but nice at the same time, to be held by a boy as we moved slowly round the room. At the end, he gave me a brief kiss on my lips and then the lights went on in the hall! I moved away from him just as he started to ask for my phone number. But he didn't have anything to write it down on! I knew my father was waiting in the car so I said I had to go. To this day, I wonder about Chris and what might have happened if he had taken my number. He really did seem like a nice boy!

Mary was worried about what her grandchildren might think when they read this (they're in their early teens themselves) but they thought it was 'very sweet'. It certainly rings bells with me; I can recall dances like that, all too well, myself!

This memory comes from Gill, another life story student.

MY FIRST BIKE

My first bike was a hand-me-down from a cousin. But I didn't mind because I was desperate for one! It was red and a bit small for me although I loved it! We lived in a town so my parents wouldn't let me ride my bike on the road. Instead, I rode it up and down the little path to our house. But I would go and stay with my cousins during the holiday on a farm they owned and I was allowed to ride one of their bikes there. The only trouble was that it was a boy's bike with a cross bar down the middle! One day, we were cycling along down an old track and I fell off. I cut my knee quite badly and had to have it stitched up – I still have the scar to prove it. But it didn't put me off bikes and when I went to university years later, the first thing I did was buy a second-hand bike to ride to lectures!'

There's some nice humour here, isn't there! Humour is always a good thing to put into your life story because it makes your reader relax and feel part of your life.

The following memory comes from Sally.

FIRST TIME THAT I WENT AWAY WITHOUT MY PARENTS

'*It was in the sixties when I was about 14. A friend of mine was going on a teenage activity holiday and asked if I could go too. I was excited because there were going to be boys there! But as the time approached, I felt quite nervous about leaving my parents. We were going to be camping but the tent we brought was really small and we had to borrow another which leaked at night. But that didn't matter because we made friends with the others and toasted marshmallows over the camp fire and sang songs. I didn't get myself a boyfriend, which was what I had hoped for, but I did make lots of friends, some of whom I still see today. When I got home, I missed the freedom we'd had of going to bed late and not having proper baths! I think that was the start of my teenage rebellion!'*

MY FIRST JOB (This is still Sally's story)

'*I decided not to go to university after A levels even though it was the seventies and lots of people did. Instead, I did a secretarial course and got a job in London so I could save up money and go to Australia for a year to visit cousins. My first job was in a magazine office which I thought would be glamorous – I got it through a temping agency. At times, it was, because I would hear the girls talking about the celebrities they'd interviewed. I would also sometimes type up their articles. At other times, it was quite dull and I was itching to get out there and do what they did! One day, one of the journalists was ill and the editor asked me to go to a press fashion show instead of her. It was amazing! I borrowed a sparkly outfit from the fashion sample cupboard and felt like the bees' knees! I met lots of designers like David Shilling and Zandra Rhodes, who were very nice to me, especially when I confessed that I wasn't a real journalist. That gave me the taste to become one instead of 'just' being a secretary so I persuaded my parents to let me do a journalism course and then went on to write for a national magazine myself.*

This is now becoming compelling reading, isn't it?

MY FIRST MARRIAGE

(This is also from Sally since I thought you might like to know more about her life. To protect her family, I have changed her name.)

I met Sam during my first month at work. He was a designer in the art department and very good looking. So good looking in fact, that I didn't think he'd be interested in me so I acted normally instead of being shy and gawky! When he asked me out for a drink, I was really surprised. I don't know if it was because I went to an all-girls' school but I didn't have a lot of confidence with boys. So when Sam asked me to marry him, only six months after we'd been going out, I just said "Yes"! This was the mid seventies when not many people lived together first. In fact, my parents would have been very shocked if we'd done that.

We had a white wedding and afterwards, a small reception in the same hall where I'd gone to my first dance! Our first home was a little rented house in south London. I loved it! I was a real home bird and enjoyed making curtains while Sam did the gardening.

Sadly, Sally's marriage broke up which was one reason why she wanted to write her life story; to get it into context. She went on to write about her First Time on her own after marriage; and then life with her second husband with whom she had two children. So you'll be glad to know, it did have a happy ending!

This memory comes from Ian.

MY FIRST TRIP ABROAD

'*People didn't catch planes as often as they do now, so when I was growing up we spent our holidays in Eastbourne near my grandparents. But when I was at university during the early seventies, some friends suggested we went to what was then Yugoslavia and we stayed in Porec. It was the first time I'd ever been on a plane and I thought it was amazing! It also seemed incredible to be with people who spoke a completely different language in wonderful sunshine. All this might sound very naïve now but believe me, it was different! Now I am lucky enough to have at least two holidays a year and I always go abroad. But nothing has been as special as that rather ordinary two star hotel in Porec just because it was my first time abroad.*'

This is fun, isn't it, because it brings across a real sense of *joie de vivre* as well as some background of the time.

SUMMARY

- The 'First' method is a short, snappy way of writing your life story.
- Begin by writing down different subject headings such as First School; First Friend; First Holiday, etc. and then see if you can remember anything about it.
- Each section can be as short or as long as you want it to be. But it will look better, when printed, if you try to make each one roughly the same length.
- You'll be surprised! As you start thinking about 'Firsts', more and more will occur to you. Your first driving lesson; your first car; your first dog; your first trip to Rome and so on!

Verdict

JAN (61)

'I loved this! It didn't feel like hard work at all because it was easy to think of ideas once you'd started. Because it's usually interesting to do something for the first time, you can also remember how you felt when you did it – whether it was excitement or fear! And that added to the flavour of the story. I included doing a parachute jump for the first time when I was in my fifties, for charity. Some of my friends were amazed because they didn't know I had done it – and my granddaughter, who was too young to remember at the time, was very impressed!'

10 *Places I have lived in...*

This is a rather nice way of telling your life story. It is structured according to the places you have lived in. If you take my own life, as an example, I was born in Harrow and lived there until I was 18. I then went to Reading University and after that I lived in Cardiff, London, Buckinghamshire, Hertfordshire and now the West Country.

So, if I was to write my own life story using this structure, I would divide it into seven sections. The first would be called 'Harrow' and then I would put the years that I lived there. I would then describe anything that I remember about Harrow at that time. I would talk about the park that was just down the road from my house and where I used to fly kites with my father and play tennis. I would also describe Old Reading near Harrow, which was a lovely spot to walk in. And I might recall the old fashioned buses that we used to get which didn't have doors but which you just leaped on!

Under my section on Reading, I would talk about the fun I had cycling to lectures and the trips we used to make to places like Sonning. Once, I decided I'd like to learn to sail on the river but it was a complete disaster and I capsized!

In the Cardiff section, I would talk about what the city was like in the seventies and the wonderful indoor market there. I would also describe Penarth, a small town outside Cardiff where I had digs. Every Sunday I used to swim in an old-fashioned swimming baths. During the week, I would take the train into work at Cardiff where I was training to be a journalist.

In the London section, I would talk about the novelty of living in Hackney, which was very different from my upbringing in London. I would describe the little square where I started married life and the excitement of the market near Mare Street.

Under Buckinghamshire, I would talk about the ups and downs of living in a remote farmhouse where it was very windy because there wasn't much shelter in that particular spot. I would describe the long farm walks and the hens I used to keep.

Under Hertfordshire, I might describe living in a pretty market town and walking along the canal where there were some lovely barges and people to talk to.

And under the West Country, I would describe what it is like to live by the sea.

This is just an outline of my life, told under the Places I Have Lived In method but hopefully it will give you some ideas.

One of the nice things about writing your life story this way is that future readers might recognise the places, even if they have changed, and might have visited them too.

GUIDELINES

If you choose to tell your life story like this, think of the following pointers.

- What big event happened there?
- Did you enjoy living there?
- What were the ups and downs?
- If you had to describe the place to a blind person, what would you say? What colours, smells and noises did you hear there?
- Who did you live with there?
- Did you have children there?
- Did you have pets there?
- Were you working/at school there?
- Have you ever been back and, if so, has it changed?

CASE STUDIES

Below are some extracts from life stories written under the Places I Have Lived In method.

GLORIA

'I was born in Jamaica during the early 1950s and our first house was a bungalow which we shared with my mother's parents and about six other relatives! There were about five of us children in one room but we had a very happy life. My parents both worked on a nearby farm but there was always someone at home when we came back from school.

The bungalow had a corrugated iron roof and a veranda running round it where my grandmother would sit in the evenings. We children would play outside until it was dark. I remember lots of banana trees and also chickens running around.

When I was ten, we moved to England. My father had gone on ahead of us and rented a three bedroom house in Staines. It was very different from the Barbados house! The rooms were bigger but they felt airless because the front door was always shut, unlike our Barbados house. And instead of fields and open spaces outside, there were roads.'

SALLY

'I don't remember much about our very first house but I do recall the house we moved to when I was about four just after the Second World War. We rented it because my father was working abroad and we needed a base in Britain. It was a rather remote cottage in Berkshire and, every night, we would hear someone laughing! It sounded like a child but we couldn't find it. When my father came back to see us, he heard the laughter too. We didn't stay long at that house because we then moved to Scotland but years later, one of my brothers told me that my father had asked at the local pub if anyone knew the history of the house. Apparently, it was well known that it was haunted by a child who used to live there years ago and laughed every night. It must have been a very happy ghost!'

CLARE

' *We lived in a suburban semi in south London during the 1960s but it was in a very friendly street. My mother and the next-door neighbour – who had children the same age as us – were always popping in and out of each other's homes. I shared a bedroom with my sister and we had bunk beds which was fun as I was on the top and could look out of the window over the road outside. The kitchen was small by today's standards but I can still remember the gas oven with its funny shaped dials on the front.*

But the house that really stands out in my mind was a cottage in the Isle of Wight where my Godmother lived. We would visit every summer and it's still the nicest house I've ever seen even though I haven't been back for some years so I don't know what it looks like now. It sat halfway between the downs (behind it) and the landslip (below) so there were lots of lovely walks. You could get down to the beach in a few minutes and I particularly loved walking down some steps to Luccombe Chine. The walls were made of dry stone and I can still see the wild flowers like Red Campion growing along them. I used to collect wild flowers and would press them in a special book and then stick them in a Wild Flower Folder. I still have it somewhere.'

NICK

' *We grew up in Cumbria in a small town near my grandparents. Everyone knew each other and my parents had lived there for years with their parents. My granddad lived next door in an identical terraced house and we were always in and out of each other's houses. He kept ferrets and I used to love playing with them. I also spent hours playing football in the park that ran along the coast. Every now and then, we would get the bus into Carlisle. I liked looking at the ruined garrison there.*'

SUMMARY

- Structuring your life story in sections, according to the places you have lived in, can be a good way of bringing back memories.

- It will also intrigue readers, especially if they know these places themselves.
- It has the advantage of bringing in lots of colour and smells.
- It might appeal to life story writers who remember images and places rather than facts.

Verdict
CATHY (38)

'I found this quite easy to write because I'm a very visual person. My dad was in the RAF so we moved around a lot in life but I can still see each house in my mind's eye. They also reminded me of different stages in my life so they provided trigger points for things I might have forgotten. For instance, thinking of the Basingstoke house we lived in, reminded me of learning to drive. I started doing my life story because one of my children had to do a 'Me and My Family' project over the summer holidays. She kept asking me questions about my life so I thought I'd write it down. Then I found I couldn't stop! I read a bit every night to my children and they are fascinated!'

Quirky ways of telling your life story that you might not have thought about **11**

I hope this book has given you several ideas on how to write your life story. But if you're still unsure, here are some rather different ones that might get you going!

RECORDING ON TAPE

Some people have wonderful voices, don't they? And when they tell their life story, part of the charm is within the inflection of their voices. I have an uncle like this and also a student. I could listen to their voices for hours. So why not?

Try taping your own life story as you tell it yourself. Or, if you're doing someone else's life story, try seeing what they sound like if they read the script or ad lib into a tape recorder. (Ad libbing is simply telling their story without writing it down first.)

The beauty of this is that you are leaving a recording of your own voice for future generations. There's nothing quite like it, as I discovered when I went to an elderly friend's funeral and listened to a recording which he had made before his death, specifically for the purpose of playing at the service. It talked about his life and what he had learned and, needless to say, he had us laughing and crying at the same time.

However, there are obvious drawbacks. The first is that technology changes. So that if you keep the tape for someone to play, they may not have the right machinery in, say, twenty or thirty years' time!

The second is that you might have to do lots of re-takes! It's very easy to stammer or not come up with the right pitch on tape. And some people find their voices sound very different on a machine. So it's crucial to do some playbacks and check you are happy.

Obviously the more professional the equipment, the better the sound is going to be. But you don't need to go to the expense of hiring a studio. You might be able to do a recording on a good quality home system. Or, alternatively, it's worth contacting a local radio station (maybe a hospital radio station) and seeing if there is anyone there who can help you.

TELLING YOUR LIFE STORY IN THE THIRD PERSON

Some people want to tell their own life story but, when it comes to it, find that it's too personal or upsetting. But they still want to go ahead, perhaps because they feel it will help them tackle issues in the past or because they want to leave a record of their life for future generations.

As I write this, I am currently writer in residence of a prison two days a week where many of my students want to write their life stories. But some, understandably, find it an ordeal to recall the things they have done or re-live things that were done to them.

So, many ask for my help in writing their life story from the point of view of the third person as though they are someone else. For instance, one of my students is a former bank robber. I'll call him Steve although that's not his real name. Instead of saying 'I started robbing banks at the age of 14 when my brother asked if I would help him,' he wrote: 'Steve was just 14 when his brother asked if he'd like to rob a bank with him'.

Writing as though he was someone else allowed 'Steve' to be more open with his feelings and also his story. It also helped the therapy he was receiving because, through asking him questions about his record, he realised how scared his victims were.

You don't have to be a bank robber to benefit from this approach but it might help you if you've been through a particularly traumatic past. I have a student who was abused as a child and she used this method and found it very helpful.

SUMMARY

♦ Do consider some different ways to write your life story:
   – recording it on tape/CD;
   – telling it in the third person.
♦ Even if you haven't thought of doing it these ways, it might be worth trying them out!

Verdict
GARY (58)

‘ *My wife suggested I wrote down my life story as I'm not renowned for talking much. I found it easier to write in the third person than the first and it helped me to describe things which I had shut away in the past.* ’

Step Five

How to Make Your Life Story Stand Out with Pictures, Colours and Smells, etc.

Pictures 12

USING PICTURES TO ADD INTEREST

Some people, when they open a magazine, will look first at
the pictures. Others will go straight to the words. In this
chapter, we're going to show you how you can make your
words more interesting if you provide 'pictures' so your life
story really stands out as a work of art as well as a piece of
unique writing.

However, these don't have to be ordinary pictures. They can
be all kinds of illustrations! It could, for example, be a
photograph of yourself as a child. It could be a sketch of a
place you used to live in. It might be an old newspaper cutting
with a birth announcement or a piece of family news. It might
be a theatre programme that you kept from a special evening
out.

Start by going back to your research. Did you find anything
visual then, such as old photographs or old birthday/
Christmas cards or even stamps that you used to collect?

If so, sort them out into small piles representing different eras
of your life. Put each pile into a large envelope or folder and
label them. Now look back over the life story you have
written, using one of the structures I have suggested. See
where you can put the illustrations.

This will partly depend on what you have used to write your
life story. If you have written it on a computer, you can print
it out and then get it bound into a book or document (see
Chapter 21 on different ways and costs of doing this).

It might be that some of your illustrations can be easily inserted into such pages. For example, a photograph or sketch or family tree.

But there will be others that are too bulky. There are two ways round this. First you could simply photograph a big item such as a theatre programme or even an outfit that reminds you of a certain time.

Or you could buy an art display folder from an art shop and use this to store programmes, etc. This could be an appendix to your life story.

Here are some examples:

MURIEL (78)

'*I still have knitting patterns that my mother had to make me clothes. So after writing my life story, I put together an art folder displaying the knitting patterns through clear pages. I also added other things from over the years, including a recipe for cherry cake that I used to make with my mother in the 1940s; her old ration card from the Second World War; and my Matriculation Certificate which was an exam we took in those days. I was surprised at how it "brightened up" my life story.*'

GEORGE (69)

'*I used to collect coins as a boy so after writing my life story, I selected some of them and put them in a special book that I got from a stationers to hold coins. Underneath each one, I wrote a couple of sentences about why that coin was important to me.*'

You could use coins to structure your life story. Select coins with dates that have a special significance for you. Then buy a book with a slot for different coins and write a page to go with it, describing what happened to you in that year. You could also do the same with stamps.

Below is a summary of the kind of visual illustrations that might be handy for your life story.

- Childish drawings.
- Old school books.
- Old school essays or poems.
- Holiday brochures.
- Old letters.
- Birth certificates.
- Marriage certificates.
- Death certificates.
- Comics.
- School reports.
- Newspaper cuttings.
- Stamps.
- Coins.
- Prospectuses from schools.
- Job awards.
- Photographs.
- House details.
- Christmas cards.
- Birthday cards.
- Baby mittens.
- Shells.
- Postcards.
- Baby teeth.
- Lock of baby hair.
- Maternity ward baby wrist identity bracelet.
- Church service sheets.
- Record covers.
- Recipes.
- Tickets from shows.
- Transit labels/airline tickets.
- Pages from a diary or year book.
- Sporting certificates.
- Pictures of sporting trophies.

SUMMARY

- A life story can look more appealing and interesting if there are illustrations.

- You can even include small objects or, if they are too big, use a special display book with pockets as an appendix to your life story.

Verdict
DENISE (49)

' To be honest, I was worried that my life story might seem a bit boring. And when I was told to look for illustrations, I didn't know where to start. But then I began looking through a box where I had stored precious things from my childhood and I found a letter from the Blue Peter *children's programme, thanking me for helping to organise a garage sale in aid of charity. So I photocopied the letter and stuck it in. Then I found a Brownie certificate to prove I had passed an exam in tying knots and that went in too! I also put a pressed flower in that I'd kept from my wedding bouquet.* '

Noises, smells, colours 13

When you read a novel, you are more likely to get hooked if there is plenty of noise, smell, colour, taste and any other 'sense' that makes you able to picture the scene being described.

The same goes for a life story. If you can describe the noises that you heard in the house you grew up in (the traffic on the road outside or the chickens in the yard), or what school smelt like (cabbage and disinfectant), you'll be more likely to encourage others to read it and keep turning those pages.

Hopefully, by now you will have finished the first draft of your life story. But now you can add these extra layers to make it even more special!

Below is a checklist of various 'senses' and tips on how you can use them in your life story.

BRINGING THE SENSES ALIVE

Noise
What kind of noises did you hear when:

- you were in your first house (footsteps in the night);
- you went to school (rowdy classrooms; strict teacher's voice; songs you sang);
- you went on holiday (animals; people talking in foreign accents);
- you started work (loud office; someone with a distinctive voice; clatter of machinery);
- you got married (sounds at the wedding; the hymns and music played);
- you had children (constant arguing! Also laughter)?

Smells

What kind of smells do you remember from:

◆ childhood (mother's cooking; mother's perfume; smell of special toy);
◆ school (new school uniform; new shoes; lunches);
◆ holiday (smell of lavender or sun tan lotion);
◆ work (stuffy air; flowers; smell of products you were working with; ink);
◆ first home (new carpets; paint);
◆ getting married (smell of a special perfume you wore on the day);
◆ having children (baby smells; baby lotions, etc.)?

Taste

◆ Taste of certain meals you remember from different stages of your life. For example, Black Forest Gateau was very popular during the 1970s.
◆ Occasions when your taste buds changed (e.g. pregnant).

Colours

◆ What was your favourite colour as a child?
◆ What was the colour of your school uniform?
◆ Or a bridesmaid dress?
◆ Or your wedding dress?
◆ Or a favourite outfit?

Touch

Can you remember how the following items felt when you touched them?

◆ Special outfit.
◆ Toy.
◆ Curtains.

HOW TO USE THIS

Below is an example from Fiona, one of my students who used some of these prompts to brighten up her life story:

' *During the Second World War, we were sent to stay with a great-aunt in Wiltshire. She smelt of mothballs and always wore long grey skirts. I was rather afraid of her but I loved being with my great-uncle. He spent most of his time in the greenhouse and I would help him. Every time I smell a chrysanthemum or tomato plant, it takes me right back to him.*

My aunt and uncle kept chickens and they made squawking noises from morning to night. Every day, I was woken up by the rooster who sounded like a siren from London!

My aunt was a good cook but I loved helping her in the kitchen even though she was very strict about hygiene! We always had to wash our hands first with soap that smelt of tar! I particularly liked helping her to make cakes and I can still smell that lovely warm mixture when it came out of the oven. Sometimes she would let me lick the spoon. I was helping her make a cake one day when my uncle came in, looking very serious. He told me that my home in London had been bombed but that luckily my parents had both been out so they were safe.

Do you see what a difference it made, by adding the different senses?

Here's another example from Gail, another student of mine:

My grandfather used to run a sweet shop in the 1950s. I used to help him on Saturdays and I loved filling up the big, heavy glass jars with boiled sweets. Sometimes he would allow me to have one and I can still taste the sticky bulls eyes! I also liked flying saucers which were made of paper in lots of different rainbow colours. They melted in your mouth, leaving you with sherbert inside. It makes my mouth water just to think of it!

SUMMARY

◆ When you've finished the first draft of your life story, go back and inject colour, noise, smell, taste and any other kind of sense you can think of.

Verdict

PAM (43)

'I was amazed at what a difference it made to add noise, colour, taste and smell to my life story. I couldn't do it for all the sections and I think that if I had, it would have been too much. But it made some of the sections come to life and sound less wooden.'

Step Six

How to Provide a Contemporary Feel to Your Life Story

Fads, gadgets and innovations 14

When an older person tells us about their life, it's always interesting to hear about things which we don't use now. Or to hear about customs and traditions that were commonplace. I personally find it fascinating to hear about crazes or trends of the time.

Similarly, if you can insert into your life story the sort of gadgets or products you used at that time, you will bring your tale to life. You'll do the same if you include customs and traditions.

By now, you will have hopefully written the first draft of your life story. Now I want you to go back and look at the different sections. Do any of the sections remind you of fads, gadgets or innovations that were new at the time?

Below is a list of ideas that might trigger some memories.

FADS

- ◆ Long johns.
- ◆ Pom pom pets.
- ◆ Sindy dolls.
- ◆ Discos.
- ◆ Hot pants.
- ◆ Mini skirts.
- ◆ Mary Quant tights.
- ◆ Trolls.
- ◆ Radio Caroline.

GADGETS AND INNOVATIONS

- ◆ Automatic washing machines.

- Colour televisions.
- Dishwashers.
- Trouser presses.
- Muesli.
- Yoghurt.
- Package holidays.
- Answerphones.
- Electric blankets.
- Telegrams.
- Fax.
- Email.

TRADITIONS

- Saturday morning cinema.
- Clementines and nuts at the bottom of Christmas stockings.
- British beach holidays.
- Pancake races.

These are just a few ideas. I am sure you can add to these yourself. It might also help to talk to other people your age to see if they can think of things too.

Below are some examples from life story students on how they have incorporated these memories into their accounts.

SYLVIA (58)

'In the 1960s, we all wore long johns to keep warm! They were like leggings but they ended at the knee. The funny thing is that they were popular with all kinds of age groups. I had a pair and so did my mother and my grandmother! They were in bright colours like reds and blues and they had a bit of lace at the bottom. Everyone had a pair!'

HUGH (70)

'I was a schoolboy during the 1950s and every Saturday, my parents would give me a coin to take my sister to the Saturday morning cinema showing. It was always a suitable film especially for children and my friends went too. Someone would come onto the stage below the screen and introduce the film which made it seem all the more exciting. I remember *taking my sister to see* Bambi *but she cried so much that I had to take her out and the manageress rang my mother.*

GEORGE (63)

' *When I was growing up, not every house had a telephone. I was very excited when we got one at the beginning of the 1950s. But you didn't just dial a number. You called 100 and asked for the operator. Then you gave her the number and she put you through. Each area had a name instead of a number. Our area was called "Grimsdyke".* '

JEAN (57)

' *I was about nine when my mother gave us muesli for the first time for breakfast. We'd never had anything like it! My father said it was rabbit food and refused to eat it but mum said it was healthy!* '

ROSEMARY (59)

' *My mother didn't work even though we didn't have much money. In those days, men didn't always like their wives working because it suggested they couldn't support them. In contrast, even though my father worked an hour away in an office, he would always be back by supper time and we would all sit up round the table which my brother and I would have laid first. Afterwards, we would help my mother wash up. My father would also go to work on Saturday mornings. It was considered quite normal!* '

SUSAN (50)

' *When I went shopping with my mother, she would always get Green Shield Stamps. It was a way of saving up for things. When you got a certain number, you could buy something like an iron! We always used to go shopping every day. There weren't any supermarkets; instead, there were individual shops like greengrocers and haberdashers. And we didn't have any frozen food.* '

WHAT WE DIDN'T HAVE – AND HOW WE MANAGED WITHOUT!

Sometimes, asking yourself what you DIDN'T have will also inspire some colourful memories.

GWYNN (70)

' *We didn't have a hair drier when we were growing up. We just rubbed our hair dry with a towel!* '

LINDA (49)

' *We didn't have a car of our own so we used to walk or get a bus. I think it made people talk to each other more. Sometimes if it was raining, complete strangers would stop to offer lifts. One day on holiday in the Isle of Wight, we were waiting for a bus when a woman in a car stopped to ask if we wanted a ride and it turned out that she and my mother had known each other years ago in Salisbury! But you also had to be careful. Once when I was a child, a man pulled up at a bus stop where I was waiting to go to school and asked if I wanted a lift because it was raining. But I said no. To this day, I get scared about that. I just knew he wasn't very nice. The other thing about cars is that lots of women didn't drive until the late 1960s. It just didn't seem that necessary; maybe because several didn't work.* '

MURIEL (59)

' *My parents wouldn't have dreamed of taking us anywhere on a plane! That was for the very rich or famous. For holidays, we used to go to Margate to stay with my aunt. We had a lovely time on the beach and in the evenings, we would play cards like whist or rummy.* '

ANNE (64)

' *In common with many people, we didn't have a washing machine of our own. So my mother used to carry bags to the launderette three times a week. She made quite a lot of friends that way. On Saturdays, we would help her. When we did get a washing machine in the 1960s, it was a really big deal! But it wasn't like the washing machines you get today. It had twin tubs so when the washing was done, you had to lift it out and put it in the other tub to spin it. Not nearly so convenient! Even then, it didn't dry it properly so we would hang it over chairs.*

SANDRA (68)

We didn't have central heating – goodness me, no! We had coal fires but only in the best room, in the evening. The rest of the time, we just put on an extra jumper. At night, instead of a hot water bottle or an electric blanket, we had brass pans which we filled with hot water or hot bricks which we wrapped in flannel.

SUMMARY

- ◆ Look back over the different stages of your life story and see if you can think of any fads, gadgets, traditions or new things of that time.
- ◆ Try to remember as much detail as possible and then put it in the relevant spot.
- ◆ Also think of things that people have today and take for granted. Did you have them too – and if not, how did you manage? This can really help a life story come to life.

Verdict

DAVID (66)

I enjoyed this – although I had to stop myself writing too much. There were so many things that we didn't have and that got me thinking about how we managed. A lot of people my age say that the world was a better place without all these inventions. But I'm glad we've got them. I don't know how I managed without email, for instance. It helps me write to my grandchildren in Australia and saves waiting for the post.

15 *Making a song and dance!*

Isn't it amazing how you can hear a tune from the past and, immediately, you are transported back in time! For me, it's 'My Old Man's a Dustman', which my grandmother used to play again and again. Because it used to make her laugh, I laughed too as a child – and simply thinking about it now – all these years later – still makes me smile.

I'd like you to do the same right now. Think of music over the years that meant a lot to you at the time. It might be a song you sang at school. Maybe a hymn. Perhaps it was a nursery rhyme. Or even a Brownie/Guide/Cub/Scout song. Perhaps it was a pop tune from your teens. Or, if you're a little older, something from the 1920s–50s.

Here are some titles to get you started

- 'Lipstick on my Collar' – Helen Shapiro.
- 'She Loves Me' – The Beatles.
- 'Jerusalem' – hymn.
- 'Whiter Shade of Pale'.
- The National Anthem.
- 'The Wedding March'.
- 'We'll Meet Again'.

HOW TO USE THEM

When you've made your list, go back to the first draft of your life story and see where they might fit in. You could either add a few lines to say that, at this time, such and such a song meant a great deal to you and then explain why. Or you could put a footnote at the end of the section and simply head it: Popular songs of the day. Then give the title.

Below are some examples of how life story students have used music in their own tales.

EMILY (79)

'*I remember singing the National Anthem at work just after the Coronation. I was about the same age as the new Queen so I suppose I felt a sort of empathy even though our lives were so different. I worked, at the time, in a factory! Anyway, someone on the shop floor started to sing the National Anthem spontaneously and we all followed suit. It still makes me feel tingly to think about it.*'

ANGELA (55)

'*I can't remember the song itself but I do remember the picture on the record sleeve for Helen Shapiro's hit 'Lipstick on my Collar'. It was in my parents' record collection and I thought the singer looked very glamorous on the cover. I didn't understand the significance of the title until I was much older!*'

SUSAN (61)

'*Anything by Ginger Rogers transports me back to the 50s! I adored her and wanted to be just like her when I grew up. My mother actually took me to see her in London and I've never forgotten it. She was so graceful! This memory inspired me to go through some of my precious things and I actually found the programme from the show so I've used it to illustrate my life story.*'

DANCE/THEATRE

Now try thinking about shows that you've been to during your life. Cast your mind back to:

- ballet performances;
- concerts;
- plays;
- pantomimes.

What did you see and who did you see it with? Was it at a pivotal (important) time of your life? What happened before the performance or after it? Did you receive a proposal or decide you didn't want to be with the people you went with?

Or, as with Pauline, 51, did you actually get asked on stage!

'*My parents took me to a pantomime in Birmingham during the sixties – Mother Goose – and at the end, the cast invited some of the children in the front rows to go up on stage with them! I didn't want to but I was with my older sister who dragged me with her! I'll never forget standing there and looking down on a sea of people with lights shining in my eyes. I couldn't even see my parents. But I came off that stage, with a strange excited feeling in my chest and I knew that even though I had been nervous, I couldn't wait to go back up again. I joined a local amateur dramatic group soon after that and have been a member ever since!*'

TELEVISION PROGRAMMES

Television programmes – and their theme tunes – always remind us of a certain stage in our lives, don't they? But it's amazing how many life story students forget to include the ones that mattered to them.

Again, you can do what you did with music. Either think of a list of programmes you remember and then insert a couple of lines about them in the relevant section of your life story. For example, if you wrote your life story in a chronological order, structuring it in different years, you might put *Watch With Mother* in the years 1950–1960. The programme itself might well have been transmitted both before and after these dates, but if you are writing your life story in ten-year chunks, that's where it would probably fit best.

Then you might write a couple of lines about what you remember about the programme. Many of us in that vintage recall Bill and Ben, the flower pot men, and how they made us laugh. You might describe how you sat on the floor and watched it at home with a brother or sister.

Or you might simply want to write a small heading after this section of your life story and put POPULAR TELEVISION PROGRAMMES OF THE TIME. Then you could list *Watch With Mother* and any others. (You can find out about them from the internet by Googling 'Television Programmes 1950–1960'.)

TRACEY (54)

' *I remember watching* The Avengers *on Friday nights! I know when it was because it was always after Guides and I was allowed to stay up late to watch it. My heroine was Emma Peel and I wanted to be just like her!* '

GARY (58)

' *It's the adverts I remember on television. I still remember that toothpaste one with the ring of confidence slogan. For me, it sums up cleaning my teeth before school and being told to hurry up by mum.* '

MY FAVOURITE BOOK WAS...

This is another – vital – way of making your life story stand out and come to life. Think back to the books you loved as a child and also in your adult years. What did your parents read to you? Were you reading a particular book at a time in your life when big events were happening?

This is what one of my students wrote:

HENRY (58)

' *When I was ten, I was sent to boarding school because my father had to work abroad and my mother went with him. I don't know how I would have survived without reading under the covers by torchlight after 'Lights Out'. One of my favourite books was* Swallows and Amazons. *I loved the idea of setting out in a boat with friends and I also liked the fact that the children were so independent! It helped me to escape school in my head. Later, I joined the Navy. I'm sure that wasn't a coincidence!* '

Here are some other book titles down the years that might trigger your memory.

- *Brer Rabbit.*
- *My Naughty Little Sister.*
- *Eric, or, Little by Little.*
- *The Yearling.*
- *The Famous Five.*
- *Our Island Story.*
- *Susannah and the Mounties.*

SUMMARY

- Always remember the power of music, theatre, television and books. They can sum up different stages of your life and will ring bells with readers.
- They also help to 'fix' your life story in a historical context.
- Start by making a list and then seeing where they fit in.

Verdict
HOWARD (43)

‘ *I loved this section! I was actually writing a life story for a surprise birthday present for my mother so I had to do quite a lot of research to find out what kind of music, plays and books were popular at the time. The local library helped and, of course, Google. My mother was thrilled with the result and it got me interested in music that I hadn't come across before. I also spoke to people of her age who helped me with their memories.* ’

How much did that cost? 16

This chapter will involve some more research – something you might or might not want to do. But I do think it is worth it! Let me explain. . .

I don't know about you but I am always fascinated to find out how prices have changed. Just take a simple loaf of bread which could, today, cost anything from 60p (roughly) to £2 or £3. But how much would it have been when you were growing up in the 1930s? Or the 1970s?

You can find out by Googling 'How much', etc. on the internet or asking someone to help you do this. Then try some other basic items and maybe some luxury items too. In fact, I suggest making a list of some basics and luxuries and seeing how much they have cost during your life. Obviously, they are going to change as you get older so try taking it in ten-year gaps. For instance, you could see how much a loaf of bread would have cost in 1940; 1950; 1960 and so on.

Then, do the same with other items so you have a final list of ten. (You could have fewer if you prefer.) At the end of each section of your life story, list the products and their prices. This will help to 'sit' your life story in a social context.

Here are some examples of things you could look up.

◆ A pint of milk.
◆ A loaf of bread.
◆ A house (depending on size, obviously).
◆ The monthly gas bill for a three bedroom house.
◆ A piece of furniture.
◆ The average wage.

OLD AND NEW MONEY!

In 1971, we had decimalisation, when the old currency of shillings and pence suddenly became new pounds and pence. If your life story included that period, it's worth adding a few lines to talk about the effect this had on your life.

Perhaps you were an adult at the time and found it hard to get used to the difference. Maybe you were a child and found it easier.

LOUISE (56)

'*I was a child when my parents started talking about something called "new money". They were worried that they wouldn't be able to understand it and that my grandmother, who was in her sixties, would have trouble. At school, we had lots of lessons explaining that we weren't going to have shillings any more but pounds and new pence. I don't remember finding it very difficult although I still find it hard to think in terms of metric when it comes to measuring things. I'm much happier with feet and inches!*'

Step Seven

Bringing the Rest of the World into Your Life Story

Writing a timeline 17

We've already talked about the importance of setting your life story in its historical and social context. The good news is that you've done a lot of work already by finding out the prices of certain items and also remembering plays and books and music from the time.

We've also talked about how you can use this research to add more colour to your life story stages. But you can also use it all again to do something else – create a timeline!

The great thing about a timeline is that it helps future readers to understand your life in terms of what was going on outside, in the big wide world. And this will make your story even more special.

This is best done either at the end of your life story or at the end of each section of your life story. And it's actually simpler than you think!

HOW TO START

Begin by writing down the dates of your life story. Start with the beginning date and then either write down each year on a separate line on a piece of paper or a chunk of years such as 1945–1950.

Then write down the following, either on the relevant line, or in the space between a chunk of years.

- Who was the Prime Minister(s) during this period?
- Were there any wars happening either at home or abroad?
- What big world events were happening?

- What breakthroughs were there – discoveries or expeditions such as the first landing on the moon?
- What did a loaf of bread cost?
- What was the average wage?
- Which celebrities were famous at the time?
- Name a popular song/film/play/book/TV programme.

HOW TO FIND OUT THE ANSWERS

Frankly, the best way in today's day and age, is the internet. Type these questions into Google and see what you come up with. If you can't do this, ask someone to help. Also go to the local library and see if someone can help in the research department.

Example of a timeline with historical events.

1948 – Beginning of the National Health Service.

1949 – UK becomes a founder member of Nato.

1953 – Coronation of Queen Elizabeth II.

1956 – Suez Canal crisis.

1961 – UK applies to join the European Economic Community but is vetoed by French President Charles de Gaulle.

1962 – The Beatles have their first Top 20 hit in the UK with 'Love Me Do'.

1969 – British troops sent to Northern Ireland.

1973 – UK joins the European Economic Community. Three-day week. Miners' strike.

1979 – Conservative politician Margaret Thatcher becomes prime minister.

Examples of prices

In 1957:

- a loaf of bread cost fourpence (about 2p today);
- a pint of beer was one shilling (5p);
- the minimum agricultural labouring wage was £7 per week;
- a dozen eggs were one shilling and sixpence (7.5p)

(Information from Ask Jeeves)

Famous bands in the 1960s

- The Rolling Stones.
- The Who.
- The Animals.
- The Beatles.

SUMMARY

- Spend some time doing research and drawing up a timeline.
- You can add this to your life story either at the end of each section or at the end.
- A timeline will put your own life into context and provide a fascinating overview of prices, celebrities and historical events.

Step Eight

How to End Your Life Story – and Make Sure That It Doesn't Hurt Anyone (Including Yourself)

How to end your story when you're still alive! 18

A strange thing happens when you get towards the end of your life story. You begin to realize that, somehow, you need to end it. But how exactly do you do that?

If someone else was writing this about you as an obituary or for a eulogy, it would be simple! It would end with your death and, we hope, several nice compliments.

But you are still alive and it's not so easy to pay yourself tributes in case it looks boastful.

Below are some suggestions on how you can end your life story on a positive, upbeat note without sounding too self-congratulatory! Take a look at some of the options and find one – or a mixture – which you like best. You might, by now, also have some ideas of your own.

A SUMMING-UP

This would be a general summing-up of how you feel your life has gone so far. You could include achievements and also disappointments. You could also talk about what you are proud of and what you wish you hadn't done in life. You might also talk about what you hope to go on and do now.

ANDREA (64)

‘ *To sum up, I am glad I re-trained as a teacher after my children went to school. It meant I could be there for them during the holidays. But I do wish I had retired earlier instead of waiting until I was 60! If I had my time again, I would have packed up ten years before that so I had more energy. On the plus side, I'm still healthy and I'm really glad that I've had the opportunity to travel. Although it was a terrible shock when my husband died, I've learned to be more independent than I thought I could be. I've also made some wonderful friends and I hope that I've been able to help out with my grandchildren too. They are a great joy to me. I've already promised to take them on my next trip abroad even though I don't know where that will be.*'

A PROFILE

This could be a summing-up in a different kind of way. You might choose to describe yourself to future generations. Although you did this briefly at the beginning, your reader will have got to know you better now. So you could talk about your career; your role in the family; your sports trophies if you have any; or anything else that you would like to be remembered for. It's a less emotional summing-up than the one in the previous section; a bit like a CV.

SYLVIE (59)

'*I seem to have had lots of different careers in my life ranging from being a secretary to a company director. But I've learned different lessons from each one. I hope that I've shown my daughter that it is possible to be a mother and have a career although there have obviously been sacrifices. Now I'm looking forward to a new challenge in setting up a new company.*'

A SPIRITUAL SUMMING UP

This might be added to the previous sections or it could stand in its own right. You might want to take this opportunity to say how you feel about the future – and life after death. You might also want to say how religion has or hasn't played a part in your life.

BELLA (49)

'*It wouldn't be right to reach the end of my life story without talking about a very recent change in religion. Until last year, I used to be Church of England but then I went to a Catholic service to keep a friend company. I was very struck by the warmth and companionship offered by the congregation and now I am training to be a Catholic myself. It has given me a great sense of peace about the future. In fact, I don't know how people manage to get through life without a faith.*'

LESSONS IN LIFE

This can be as light or as serious as you want. Future generations are often keen to find out the meaning of life and this is your chance to tell them what you have learned. You might say that you wish you'd paid more attention to keeping tax records. Or that you wish you'd spent more time with your family. Or you could say you wish you'd spent more time on the football field... The list is endless.

LISA (59)
'*I wish I'd been a rebellious teenager. Writing my life story has shown me that I was a rather boring, good child! Maybe it's now time to rebel especially now I've had a birthday milestone!*'

SAYINGS

I rather like this idea. Some of my students have chosen to write down sayings that have helped them through life. Here are some examples:

GEOFF (41)
'*Live for the moment.*'

LOUISE (37)
'*Don't put things off. Face the facts.*'

JANE (54)
'*Follow your gut instinct and listen to that little voice inside you that says "Do" or "Don't?" or "Don't trust him or her". Ignore it at your peril!*'

SAM (53)
'*Don't get hooked on your emails.*'

NEIL (30)
'*Just do it. Whatever it is.*'

POEMS

Another rather nice way to finish off. You could choose a poem that has meant a lot to you and quote from it (make sure you mention the author and that you have checked if you need permission to do this).

Personally, I think it is nice to make up your own poem. Here's an example by one of my maturer students.

JOHN (76)
'*This is my life; this is my tale;*
This is my boat on which I shall sail.
So when I'm gone, I will still live on
Through my story entitled "The life of John"!'

Even if you've never tried before, you might want to have a go. Try to think of lines which end in words that you can easily rhyme with others.

For instance:

> '*Today is the day when Bert turns sixty eight.*
> *So we thought we'd write his story before it's all too late!*'

'Eight' and 'late' are obvious rhymes, although I hope that Bert is the kind of chap who will take this in good spirit!

When trying to think of a rhyme for a word, go through the alphabet and see what works. For instance, if you were trying to think of a rhyme for 'eight', you might consider 'bait', 'date,' 'fate', 'gate' and so on.

I think the trick, in writing a life story in rhyme, is to select five or six main events in someone's life and dedicate one or two or maybe more verses to each one. Let's go back to Bert, who was in the army.

> *'It wasn't long before he got some stripes upon his sleeve.*
> *And all the pretty girls in town looked forward to his leave!'*

Poems like this can work particularly well if you are writing a life story for a special occasion such as a birthday or retirement when it's good to have a laugh. It might not work so well, however, as a eulogy when people are feeling more solemn.

MESSAGE FOR FUTURE GENERATIONS

If you were suddenly propelled in time to The Future and met your great-great-great-grandchild, who then asked you to describe your life in just one sentence, what would you say?

Yes – it's a tough one! But it might help you to concentrate your thoughts if you know you only have one sentence. Here's what one of my students said:

ANNA (61)
'It was a great ride!'

MY HOPES FOR THE FUTURE

This can be interesting because it forces you to think about what you want to do next. Sometimes, writing a life story can help people focus on what they really want to tackle. Or it might make them realise that they have been so busy until now, that they need a bit of a rest!

HOWARD (45)
'I've decided now that I've spent most of my life doing what other people have expected me to do. I began this life story when I was made redundant and my therapist suggested I kept busy by writing about the past. Now I am going to sell my house and move to the sea. Maybe I will get a dog. Who knows? But I feel much more positive about life. I've decided not to show anyone my life story because it contains quite a

lot of personal stuff. But every now and then, I will get it out and remind myself of how far I have progressed.

IT'S YOUR FUNERAL!

Another fun exercise. Imagine you are at your own funeral. What would you like the person who is giving the eulogy to say about you? Write it down. This is your chance to describe yourself, warts and all.

ANON (MAYBE NOT SURPRISINGLY!)

She was never on time, mainly because she had impossible expectations of herself and thought she could do it all! She never stopped talking but she was also highly entertaining and could tell a good joke even if it was at her own expense. Oh – and she was hopeless with both money and men. She got through both, at a prodigious rate!

GOOD ADVICE

When my mother died in her fifties, she left me a scrap of paper with a poem in beautiful Victorian copperplate writing. It has given me a lot of strength over the years and also to other people to whom I've showed it. In fact, I'd like this on my gravestone one day. Here it is:

Weeping for the past is useless.
Weeping for the present merely clouds your eyes
so you see less clearly into the future.

Ouch! The importance of thinking about other people's feelings

19

Writing your life story can seem like an innocuous thing to do. What is wrong, after all, in writing about your own life. It belongs to you, doesn't it?

In fact, your family history might well contain skeletons that would upset others in the family if they were put into print. So do be careful before you launch straight in.

Strangely enough, you might be surprised at how you can all too easily upset someone by mentioning things that may not seem sensitive to you but are to other people.

'One of my sons was put out because he thought I mentioned his sister's achievements more than his,' said one of my students recently.

Another one said that her family felt threatened when she said she was going to write her life story. 'I told them I just wanted to write down family stories so they would remember them when I was gone. But in the end, I had to promise I would show it to them before I had it printed. They actually liked it but I was surprised by their initial reaction.'

Personally, I think that if you are going to pass your life story around the family during your lifetime, it is a good idea to show what you have written to the people you have mentioned.

The alternative is to put it in your bottom drawer and leave them to discover it at a time when you won't be around. But even then, you could cause offence.

This doesn't mean you shouldn't write your life story. But do try to be diplomatic!

There's another person you need to consider too, when writing your life story. And that's yourself! Sometimes, it can be surprisingly painful to write about the past. It can bring back old memories, which you thought you had buried, or feelings that you thought you had got over. But now, on writing them out, you might find that they surfaced again.

If you find it very upsetting, it might be time to stop or to face your fears. I'd suggest talking to an expert such as your doctor or a friend or counsellor if that happens to you. On the other hand, you might also find that writing about something which has troubled you in the past is actually very healing.

Rose (not her real name) came to me when she was in her retirement to write about her life. But when we reached the part where she had been treated for breast cancer during her fifties, she burst into tears. 'In fact, this was the best thing I could have done. At the time, I had to hide my fears and grief over my mastectomy because I didn't want to upset my husband or children. But by writing about it, I felt released and lighter.'

Writing a life story for someone else 20

So far, we've concentrated on how to write your own life story and the reasons for doing it, but writing a life story for someone else can be a wonderful idea. It might be:

- a surprise birthday present;
- a retirement present;
- a lengthy eulogy at a funeral;
- a commission (for which you are paid).

HOW TO GO ABOUT IT

If you are going to write a life story for someone as a surprise, it's vital to get your facts right. It would be awful if you wrote something that was inaccurate – even the spelling of someone's name could spoil the gift or certainly make it look as though you hadn't done your homework.

My advice is to arm yourself with a notebook and possibly a tape recorder and interview as many people as you can about the life story subject. Try to find interviewees who have been part of different sections of the subject's life. Someone from their work. A relative. A friend. A neighbour. Maybe the local vicar. Explain why you're doing this, but if it's a surprise do tell them in case they inadvertently let on! It's also a good idea to read back what you've written to the interviewee so they can check they are happy with what they have said and to make sure that you have written it down correctly.

You could also Google the person you are writing about, but there is no certainty that the information will be accurate.

If you're not used to interviewing people, here are some questions you could put to them.

- When did you first meet the life story subject and what were your first impressions?
- Has that person changed over the years and, if so, how and maybe why?
- What qualities has the life story subject shown e.g. kind; loyal? Can they give examples of that? This might lead to some interesting anecdotes. For example, maybe the life story subject helped someone in time of distress, either by lending them money or rescuing them from an accident.
- What are the good points about the life story subject and what are their weaknesses? This can lead to some humour. For instance, I wrote a short life story for a great-aunt to celebrate her 90th birthday and I included the fact that she smoked ten cigarettes a day and enjoyed her daily tipple of malt whisky – something she tried to keep quiet from the younger generation.
- What sort of changes has the life story subject seen over the years? This depends on how old they are, but it could include some big events such as a change of monarchy. Are there any stories that your interviewee remembers about these changes?
- What anecdotes has the life story subject told your interviewees about his/her life?
- What, in the eyes of the interviewees, has made the life story subject such a special person?

You can see that, by now, you will probably have accumulated quite a lot of information. You may well need to add your own research. For instance, it would be a good idea to look up historical events during the life of your life story subject. You could also include a timeline and many of the other suggestions from previous chapters.

I think it would be nice to add a picture of your life story subject. When I did my great-aunt's story, I found an old sepia photograph of her as a child in a Victorian dress and hat which I used as the frontispiece.

The length of your life story for someone else may not be as long as your own life story – simply because you won't have so much material. But that doesn't matter. In my view, a short life story is a perfect personal present for someone because it is unique and individual.

However, if it is a surprise, do be careful that you don't say something that might offend. What might seem funny to you (and possibly true) could hurt feelings. I have one student who wrote a life story about his brother and referred to the fact that he was tight with money. Everyone laughed – apart from the brother himself.

WRITING A LIFE STORY AS A COMMISSION

This is a completely different ballgame! More and more people are advertising themselves as writers of life stories – but how can you be sure that you are going to find someone who will do a good job? Similarly, if you fancy the idea of writing someone's life story for money, how can you ensure you are professional and satisfy the client's brief?

Let's start by looking at this from the point of view of someone who is looking for someone else to write their life story. I would suggest asking the following questions:

◆ What kind of writing experience do you have?

You need to make sure this is relevant. A journalist usually makes a good life story writer because they are used to asking questions.

◆ Have you written anyone's life story before?

This isn't totally essential; after all, everyone has to start somewhere. But if your life story writer has never done it before, I would suggest asking them to write a trial chapter to make sure you are both happy. It would only be fair to pay for this but make sure you set a realistic sum. The average rate is between £20 and £40 an hour at the time of writing.

◆ How do you suggest doing it?

Some life story biographers prefer to do several sessions in which they interview the life story subject and then write it up afterwards. Others encourage the life story subjects to write their own memories and anecdotes which they will then edit and put into a readable order.

To be honest, this depends on your own personality and how much time you have – as well as how good you are at remembering things from the past. Some people, like Brian, below, found it easier to be prompted by questions:

'I thought I could just jot down memories and hand them over to the life story writer but I kept putting it off because I have such a busy job. Then, when I did get round to it, I couldn't think of anything interesting to write. So my life story writer came round to the house and asked me some key questions that I hadn't thought of before such as what I was afraid of as a child and what my biggest achievement was when I was a teenager. That made for a much more interesting read!'

A middle road approach is for the life story writer to give the subject a list of questions about their life and get them to fill in a questionnaire. From that, they have the framework of a life story and can add to it in subsequent meetings.

Such questions might include:

- Can you remember any of your birthday parties? What games did you play?
- Describe a family summer holiday.
- When did you first fall in love?
- How did you feel when you started your first job?

You'll see that I haven't just asked for facts in the questions above: I've also included feelings because that's what makes a life story work.

COST

As I've said, most life story writers will charge between £20–£40 a session. However, it might be difficult for both of you to judge how long it is going to take. I would, therefore, suggest capping the price; in other words, setting a fixed fee. Depending on the writer's experience, a life story will probably, on average, cost you anything between £200 and £1000 and that may not include the printing costs.

Summary

+ Writing someone else's life story can be a great surprise present.
+ It can also be a good way to mark someone's special birthday or retirement or even death.
+ If you are a competent writer and interviewer, you could also become a life story writer.

Verdict
Pamela (80)
'I paid someone to write my life story and it was worth every penny! Without someone to coax the stories out of me, I doubt that I would have finished it. I wanted to write it as a record of my life for my granddaughter and I gave it to her for her 21st. She said she would keep it for ever.'

Step Nine

How to Present Your Life Story and Get It Published

Presentation and getting it printed 21

Fantastic! You've finished your life story. It's been hard work – a real commitment on your part and whoever has been helping you do it. But the great news is that you have completed a real challenge and, hopefully, a challenge in life. You'll also have created a work of art which future generations will treasure. And you will have the satisfaction of knowing that you have left behind a memento that will serve as a historical 'brick' in the period of time in which you've lived.

But now what? You might well be feeling at a bit of a loss. After all, you've been working on this for months and maybe even years. Now it's over, you might be wondering what to do with your time. Or what you are going to do with your life story.

Don't panic! This is where the next stage of your life story comes in. And trust me on this, writing it is just the beginning. Now we need to focus on how to present it and how to get it published.

PRESENTATION

This partly depends on what you intend to do with your life story. If you are intending to give it to someone as a special gift, I would suggest getting it bound. There are different ways of doing this, which I will go into in a minute. But briefly, you could pay a printer to put a plastic see-through sheet on the front and then bind the left-hand edge with a plastic edging. This can usually be done for about £5 a copy.

If, however, you are hoping to get it printed and sold to a bookshop, you need to send the opening three chapters and a synopsis to an agent. Again, I will go into details, as well as the pros and cons of this, below.

However, the one golden rule is that whichever option you go for, you MUST get your life story typed. I do get some students who give me their life stories in their own handwriting. Sometimes this is legible and sometimes it isn't! It is true that handwriting adds another perspective to the writer; it makes it more individual and it can also suggest qualities about the writer. But so that it survives down the years, I would suggest that you also type it up or get someone to type it up for you. By all means include a handwritten version yourself – especially if you are writing your life story for someone else. But it is essential to have a typed alternative.

BOUND COPIES

Ring up about three local printers – you can find their numbers in *Yellow Pages* under Desk Top Publishers or Printers – and ask for quotes on binding your story. If you haven't typed your story, they might be able to recommend a typist too or you could look under Secretarial Services in *Yellow Pages*.

If your work is already on a computer, you need to save it on a memory stick and take that down to the printers. (If you don't know how to do that, ask a younger friend for help. In my opinion, the younger the better as it's the children/teens who seem to know how to do this sort of thing!) You could also email your life story to a printer.

Make sure you include a cover page for your life story so it doesn't launch straight into your book. For instance, you could write something like this:

> THE LIFE STORY OF EVELYN SMITH.
> Born 1931 and now aged 69.
> This was written in 2010 to be read by future generations.

I would also look out a picture of yourself from an early age. If you can find one where the clothes and hairstyle are reminiscent of the time, even better! You might also want to find a current picture of yourself. Send these to the printer (either by post or by hand) and ask if he can copy these and put it on the title page.

Also ask for a second copy, either for yourself or as a spare.

After that, it's up to you to decide what to do with it. Some of my students have simply put it in a bottom drawer for their families to find. Others have given it to their family immediately. And some have left it with their lawyer along with their wills!

IS MY LIFE STORY GOOD ENOUGH TO BE SOLD IN A BOOKSHOP?

Several of my students hope that their life stories might become a bestseller. And indeed, some life stories have done exactly that! Look at *Angela's Ashes* by Frank McCourt, which told the story of his poverty-stricken childhood in New York and Ireland.

However, we also need to be realistic. Nowadays, there's an enormous trend in writing life stories. And they can't all be sold in Waterstones. On the other hand, there are always exceptions...

A life story is more likely to stand a chance with an agent and/ publisher if:

◆ it is written by a celebrity;
◆ it is written by someone who is close to a celebrity;
◆ the subject matter is topical;
◆ it has an important place in history;
◆ it catches the public's attention.

Call the Midwife is an example of the latter. Author Jennifer Worth has described how she decided to write about her experiences as a midwife (Merton Books, 2002).

HOW TO CONTACT AN AGENT AND/OR PUBLISHER

If you do decide to try to get your life story published and sold in a bookshop, you need to attract the interest of an agent or publisher. The first step is to get hold of a copy of *The Writers' and Artists' Yearbook* or *The Writer's Handbook*: both list agents and publishers and a great deal more.

Now I'm afraid it's a matter of guesswork, luck and talent. Select six to ten agents – avoiding those who say they don't deal with life stories or who declare they don't take unsolicited manuscripts – and send the first three chapters of your life story together with a synopsis.

A synopsis will describe, from beginning to end, what happens in your life story. It won't keep the reader guessing by saying 'And what happens in the end – read it and find out!'. It will simply outline the different stages of your life, hopefully in a way that makes the agent want to read it. For instance, if you started life as a convent girl and then went on to become a nun but gave it up to be a pole dancer, it might make an agent read on.

A synopsis also needs to say:

♦ why your life story is different;
♦ what makes your life story stand out;
♦ why your life story should be published;
♦ what your background is.

If an agent likes the look of your synopsis, they will then send it to publishers with whom they have built up contacts.

Alternatively, it is possible to send your life story to a publisher direct. Nowadays, most publishers won't look at manuscripts that don't come through an agent. This is because they rely on agents to filter out stories which aren't suitable. On the other hand, life stories fall between two stools. Some publishers will look at them and others won't. Again, it's a matter of going through *The Writers' and Artists' Yearbook* or *The Writer's Handbook* and picking some out. They won't all say if they take life stories so you will have to chance your luck.

Never email directly – always send them in the post. Address them to an editor at the publisher or a name from the agency. You can get names by ringing them up and asking for someone who specialises in life stories or checking on the internet.

SELF PUBLISHING

There are several self-publishing firms and individuals who can help you get into print. However, you will have to pay for it. The cost depends on: how long your life story is; whether there are illustrations; whether it is already edited or if you need the self-publishers to do that for you; whether you also want them to handle publicity, and so on. Therefore it's almost impossible to put an average figure on it. I know students who have paid anything between £150 to over £1000.

You can also pay for what is known as an ISBN number, which means your book is formally registered and could be sold through bookshops, provided you can persuade a bookshop to stock it. Some local bookshops are prepared to sell life stories by local authors but it depends on the story and you as a person. Try talking to the local bookshop manager to see if they are interested. And remember to talk to independents as well as chains.

Useful self-publishing contacts
The Book Guild
Author House
www.lulu.co.
www.blurb.com

You will also find editorial services advertised in the back of magazines such as *Writers' News*, *Writing Magazine* and *Writers' Forum*.

MAGAZINES

If you want to make money from your life story, you should definitely consider the magazine market. Magazines, nowadays, feed on real life stories. They simply can't get enough – and the more extreme, the better.

However, the bad news is that they won't be interested in a book because that would be far too long. What they are looking for is an idea that could be made into a one- or two-page feature which amounts to between 800 and 2000 words.

If you don't mind the idea of your life story being re-written as an article, find out who the features editor is on a magazine and then email them the idea. For example, I had a student who discovered she had psychic powers. So she sent a pitch to a magazine that ran like this:

> I wondered if you were interested in running an article about my life. I have spent most of my adult years bringing up my three children. But I kept having dreams that always came true. Sometimes they were about silly things such as finding a lost scarf. Sure enough, it was under a wardrobe just as I had dreamed it. And sometimes they were about big things such as my sister emigrating to Australia. I went to see a psychic who told me that I had magic powers myself. Now I help people see into the future.

This particular student sold her story to a woman's magazine and earned over £400!

Problems and solutions when writing your life story 22

I hope this book has solved many of your questions already. But the following common problems – and solutions – might also help.

PROBLEM

I started to write my life story but then I stopped. I had too many other things to do and I kept meaning to pick it up again but never did.

ANSWER

Set yourself goals and then stick to them! Tell yourself that you will write for half an hour every day. Or if you can't manage that, an hour every weekend. You'd be surprised at how the words will build up. It's like reading a book but only picking it up every now and then. You lose the thread as a reader. Exactly the same happens when you are the writer too. Writing small and often is better than trying to write big chunks every now and then.

PROBLEM

I keep feeling that my life story is boring. Nothing big has happened to me so far!

ANSWER

Are you sure? Sometimes things that don't seem big to you can be really interesting to others. Perhaps you remember what it was like to be a teenager during the Second World War. That might have been the norm for you but it is an unknown experience for teenagers today. Or perhaps you remember when Diana, Princess of Wales, died. Your account of where you were at the time will be fascinating to future generations of readers. So don't undersell yourself! And remember that it's the little details which can make a story sing.

PROBLEM

I need to do some research to make sure my life story is correct. But I also want to start writing. Which should I do first?

ANSWER

Personally, I'd do a bit of research to get enough facts together to start writing. And then I'd write a couple of chapters. If you need to do more research for the rest, do so. But then go straight back to the writing. It's easy to do too much of one and not enough of the other so try to get a good balance. Some writers get so addicted to research that they spend years doing just that and not touching the keyboard or picking up a pen. They almost use the research as an excuse for not writing. This is why I have suggested the sandwich technique at the beginning of this paragraph!

PROBLEM

I've accumulated so much research and facts and figures that I don't know where to start!

ANSWER

Sounds like it's time to get organised. Try dividing your research into different piles. This could be according to dates, for example. So you would put everything that belongs to your early childhood in one pile and then everything in your teen years in another, and so on. You don't have to buy expensive folders for this: try using large old envelopes instead and then mark them clearly on the outside with a marker pen. By the time you've done this, you'll feel better!

PROBLEM

I thought I'd use the chronological approach in writing my life story but found that I was still on the 0–10 year stage after over a hundred pages! Should I have made this section shorter? I feel as though my life story is going to go on for ever.

ANSWER

If you are enjoying writing your life story, I'd keep going. Concentrate on the subject and don't worry about the length. My advice is to write your first draft and then put it away for a few weeks so you go back to it with a fresh eye. Then re-read it and cut out anything that is repetitive or boring.

PROBLEM

I am worried that my life story is going to upset certain members of my family. There are some personal points in it but if I cut them out, it will spoil the flavour of the story.

ANSWER

This is a very common problem and to be honest, there are no easy answers. However, there are some solutions which you might want to consider. If you are hoping your book will be published so anyone can read it, you might well change your name. If the book is designed just for your family, you might take out the bits that could hurt people. Or you could write a very honest introduction, saying that this book might contain some upsetting material but that you felt it was important to include it. You may also choose to hide the book and ask someone to reveal it after you have died – although this still might hurt those who are living. Or you might simply write the book for yourself and never show it to anyone. Sometimes, the mere act of writing your own life story for yourself can help you deal with past issues in your life.

PROBLEM

I've tried to get a publisher interested in my book but I've had countless rejections. What should I do next?

ANSWER

Unfortunately, it is difficult to get a book published in today's market. Some life stories are published but these are usually those of celebrities or of someone with an extraordinary tale to tell. There are also some amazing life stories out there that are very special but which don't make it – simply because publishers and agents are being inundated with scripts. It's a bit like a good actor or actress trying to get a role: we can't all succeed. However, the good news is that you can self-publish your book (see Chapter 21). It doesn't mean that the whole world will see it but you can sell your book privately and also try to get interest through approaching local newspapers and specialist magazines such as *Writing Magazine* to try to get someone to write a piece about your life story. This will raise the publicity profile and might even result in an editor picking it up and offering a publishing deal.

Step Ten

Still Stuck?
Tried and Tested Remedies

Writer's block 23

STILL STUCK? MORE TIPS TO HELP YOU WRITE YOUR LIFE STORY

It's your funeral!

Pretend you are at your own funeral. This isn't as depressing as it might sound. In fact, you can have fun with this one. What would you like people to say about you at your funeral? Would it be that you were a dedicated parent? Or a brilliant table tennis player? Or that you always wanted to write a novel?

Your life story in 50 words

If you're sitting there, wondering what to write, imagine that someone has given you only 50 words to describe your life. Fifty words is not impossible, is it? We have to think of five big events that have happened to us and use one sentence to describe it. Here's an example from one of my students.

> I grew up in Scotland where my sister was also born.
> I didn't enjoy school so left at 16 to become a nurse.
> At 21, I got married and went on to have three children.
> When I was 47, my marriage broke up and my children had all left home so I got a job in Holland.
> I met someone else and now I am a granny and a step-granny too!

As my student says: 'Writing those five sentences gave me the framework for a much longer book. As you can see, I actually went over the 50 word mark but that was good because it showed me that I could write much more. It also helped me to structure the book because my five sentences marked different phases in my life.'

You could also try the same but writing your life story in 100 words or 500 words or 1000. Hopefully, that will get you going so you want to write even more. . .

Tell me your secret

People love secrets! Are there any secrets in your life – or in your family that might provide more colour for your life story?

Neighbours

What kind of neighbours did you have as a child? Did you have joint firework parties? Did you play with the children next door? We used to live next to a wonderful couple whom we called Aunt Maude and Uncle Arthur. They didn't have any grandchildren so they used to ask my sister and me over to help make fudge! I have lots of fond memories of them – and you might have something similar.

Grandparents

What do you remember about your grandparents? You may have been young when they died but you might still recall their smell or things they did with you. Perhaps they have left you things that remind you of them. My grandmother left me a music box and every time I play it, it reminds me of the times I used to sit with her on her sofa and chat.

If you never knew your grandparents, try to find someone who does remember what they were like. Then you could say 'My grandfather died before I could remember him, but I have been told that. . . etc.'.

Bullies

Were you ever bullied as a child? This might not be a particularly nice memory to recall but it would certainly bring your life story to life, so to speak! I had one life story student who told me about being at boarding school in the 1950s. It wasn't a good time for him but it helped him to recall some of the things that the older boys did to the younger ones because it allowed him to release anger which he had suppressed. It also made for fascinating reading.

School trips

Do you remember the excitement of school trips? Going on a coach and having a whole day away from the classroom? Try to think of school outings that gave you that tingle and then write as much as you can about them. One of my students remembers going to The Natural History Museum in London. Unfortunately, she got left behind when the school coach went and the teacher had to come back for her. At the time, she was mortified, but as an adult, she could see the funny side. And it made a fun anecdote in her life story.

Arguments

No one likes arguments but they can definitely pep up a life story. Think of arguments you have had with people and arguments you have witnessed. One of my students remembers a silly tiff with his sister when they were children which resulted in her throwing a ruler at him. It hit his face and their mother had to rush them to hospital. He still has the scar to prove it – but it made a piece for his life story!

Getting into trouble

Have you ever got into trouble – either as a young child or an adult? If so, this might be something you could include to inject some colour. It might be being told off by a teacher, or by a boss or traffic warden or worse! Over to you...

STORIES TO INSPIRE YOU!

Below are extracts from people's real life stories. Some of the names have been changed to protect family but they are all true.

SAM'S STORY

Sam used the chronological method to tell her life story, dividing it into ten-year chunks. This is taken from the section entitled 1980–1990.

I always thought I was the only girl in my family. I joined the police – where my dad also worked – and when I went for my interview, there was a girl – I'll call her Carol – who looked very similar to me. We joined on the same day and became very good friends. We had very similar interests and even kept ferrets which was surely unusual for young girls in their twenties.

People used to say we were like sisters and at times, the similarities did seem uncanny. But I didn't take her back to meet my mum because I always knew my dad was a bit of a rat and occasionally I did wonder if we were related. When my dad died a few years later, there were a lot of people at his funeral from work and I couldn't help noticing that Carol seemed more upset than duty called for.

Soon afterwards, she came round with some pictures of a Christmas family gathering. There was a little girl in the picture – her – and my dad. Then she told me that she was my sister and that my dad had had a relationship with her mum. Apparently she'd known for a long time because our father had told her. (He came from farming stock which was why we'd both been interested in ferrets – it was in our genes.)

I'm sorry to say that I was so upset that I shunned Carol after that and didn't want any more to do with her. This upset her. By then I was married and my husband and I moved to the country. I told my friends that I didn't want Carol to have my new address.

Then, a few years later, we were coming back from Dorset and it was exactly 9.10pm on the clock. I said to my husband 'When we get back, I'm going to ring Carol'.

He said 'Don't be silly. It's too late.'

But I was determined. However, as soon as we got into the house (by then it was just gone 10pm), the phone rang. It was a friend who said she wanted me to be the first to know. Carol had been killed in a car crash at exactly 9.10pm that night. She'd gone into a farm vehicle and her neck had been broken. The awful thing is that ever since I was 16, I'd been having these dreams about being killed in a car crash but it was me in the car and not my sister. It almost put me off having children.

I'd like to think my sister has forgiven me. Her death has

partly inspired me to write my life story to try and make sense of it all.

SIMANTEL'S STORY

Simantel chose to write about a specific event in her life, focusing on the year 1943. However, she was then inspired to carry on and write about life after that. You'll see that she has included lots of lovely detail including smells and colour. At times, it reads like a short story with dialogue.

The most frightening journey of my life began on a grey overcast morning in July of 1943, shortly after my fifth birthday and the beginning of my school days. The events of that day are indelibly imprinted on my mind, these are the images I still see, and this is what I remember.

Overwhelmed, and numbed by confusion, I found myself, along with hundreds of other children, marching in pairs along London's bomb-damaged streets. The scenes of devastation worsened as we neared the centre of the city.

A dusty pall hung over everything and evidence of heavy bombings and fires lay scattered in piles all around. The acrid, damp smell of burned-out buildings, some still smouldering, filled the air, the density of it made breathing difficult and my eyes watered.

Remnants of walls stood sentinel, and like accusing fingers, pointed at the open sky, awaiting the next downpour of terror. Those broken walls with wallpaper remnants flapping in the breeze had once been family homes. Their broken windows, like blinded eyes, stared out at us; shattered by explosion, they waved tattered flag-like remnants of curtains at our passing parade. I wondered where the families were now; were they dead?

A mangy – or perhaps burned – cat emerged from a tangle of rusty bedsprings lying in the gutter. Limping, it followed us for a while, meowing. I wanted to stop and pet him, but already having difficulty keeping up with the others – I believe I was one of the youngest – I couldn't afford to lag. My legs ached and I began wondering if we'd ever get to where we were going.

At last, ushered into one of London's cavernous railway stations, a sense of relief seemed to ripple through our ranks. Perhaps now, we'd be allowed to rest for a while.

Around my neck, flapping on the end of a piece of string, I wore a brown paper label bearing my name and identity number. I stood there, a few personal belongings in a small homemade case clutched in one hand; a newspaper-wrapped parcel containing jam sandwiches in the other. My red and blue 'Mickey Mouse' gas mask, in its cardboard container, hung from my shoulder.

The previous day, kneeling on our stone-cold kitchen floor, Dad, with tears running down his hollowed cheeks, fashioned the little case from odd bits of plywood. We had no real luggage, but he had done his best, using the only available materials. He made the handle from a piece of leather, which he'd cut from his own belt.

Sniffing, he wiped a drip off the end of his nose with the back of his hand.

'I can't have her carryin' her belongin's in a paper bag, can I,' he said. Mum gave no response, she just sat watching, and I wondered why she was so quiet.

I have no recollection of saying goodbye to my family or of anyone coming to see me off at the railway station. I believe the actual day and details of our departure had to be kept a secret until the last minute. We were supposed to bring our cases to school each day and be prepared to leave on short notice. I suppose we were lucky, to be told a day in advance.

'I would 'ave died of shame if you'd gone off in dirty knickers,' Mum said.

My next memory is of fear, as faceless strangers herded us, like cattle, towards waiting train carriages. Feeling dwarfed among dozens of noisy, scruffy children, many of them sobbing and screaming for their mothers, I was too confused and frightened to cry. Who were all these children and why were some of them so dirty?

Although it wasn't Saturday, I had taken a bath the night before, and had my hair washed.

One of the boys standing close to me had scabs all over him. Terrified I'd have to sit next to him on the train, I scooted further away.

I learned later that most of the children came from London's poorest slums, that they were even poorer than we were. Many had already lost their families and homes, and had suffered worse hunger, fear and neglect than I could ever have imagined. My thoughts were all questions. What are we doing here and where are we going? The noise was deafening, my throat ached, I wanted to drop everything and run. Instead, turning my small wooden case on end, I sat and waited.

I had been placed in the care of a twelve-year-old girl named Eileen Harvey. She lived around the corner from us on Maxey Road, right next to where a bomb had left a crater in the street. Now my only connection with the world I knew and understood, Eileen became my lifeline; the lifeline I now clung to as we were ushered forward.

Before boarding the train, I stopped mid-steps for a moment and looked up at the great black steam engine. It belched out thick stinking smoke from one chimneystack, and steam hissed menacingly from another as it waited to take its bewildered occupants on their strange journey. I could almost feel the locomotive's impatience to get under way; it reminded me of a horse at the starting gate of a race, pawing at the ground. Suddenly, through the fog of bewilderment and smoke, I thought of my granddad. Didn't he work at a railway station? Might this be the one? Could he be here somewhere, looking for me? I stood on tiptoe, straining to see over the crowds. Maybe – just maybe – this was one of his trains. But then, signalling its readiness, the shrill scream of the engine whistle pierced my thoughts. I mounted the last step and entered the carriage, while behind me the sound of compartment doors slamming destroyed my brief moment of hope.

After much jostling and elbowing, Eileen found us two seats together. She shoved our belongings onto the overhead luggage rack, and me onto the seat. Clinging to her hand and snuggling as close to her as possible, I leaned my head back against the dirty red velvet seat cover. Then, feeling the powerful forward movement of the chugging steam engine, my eyes closed and I escaped into sleep.

I remember nothing more of the journey until Eileen shook me awake as the train, now almost empty, pulled into a small dark station. I have no recollection of stops along the way to drop off groups of children, nor of changing trains, as surely we must have, at least once, to get here, wherever here was.

We pressed our noses to the window, straining to see where we were. With no lights visible outside, it was impossible to see anything, except our own miserable reflections staring back at us.

At last, with the squeal of metal-on-metal brakes, we clanked to a complete stop. Standing children fell back into their seats. For a moment, there was an eerie silence. I sat there, looking from face to face, searching for clues and wondering, now what?

A woman came striding through the long train carriage shouting orders.

'Gather your things, children. Quickly now. Single file. Follow me.'

We scrambled to obey, dragging baggage and our weary selves after her, off the train. I walked behind Eileen, clinging to the belt on the back of her coat so there would be no chance of her leaving me behind.

'For God's sake stop pullin' on me. I ain't going nowhere without you,' she snapped at me over her shoulder.

Once off the train, we huddled together on the station platform until the woman in charge regrouped us into pairs. She marched this last group of tired, bedraggled children out of the station into the awaiting darkness.

After struggling with our belongings up a long steep hill, with aching arms and legs, and bellies begging for food, at last we were led into a dimly lit church hall.

Once inside, a stern-looking man, and a woman wearing a funny black hat with a long feather sticking straight up, made us stand in a line around the edge of the room. The man had a big moustache; he reminded me of walrus that was wearing a suit and tie.

'Someone will be coming to take you home shortly,' he told us, which confused me. Why would we be going home again, so soon after coming all this way? It wasn't long before I discovered he was referring to our 'new' homes.

People from the village began to arrive. They looked as apprehensive as I felt. Each of them walked up and down the line of children and began choosing whom they would take into their homes. None of them looked eager to make a selection. I was terrified that no one would want me, but that wasn't my only fear.

'Don't go without me Eileen, please don't leave me here by meself Eileen,' I begged.

'Shuddup,' she said. 'Stop whinin'.'

After what seemed an eternity, a woman, with a black-fringed shawl wrapped around her, stopped in front of me. She beckoned to the man in charge.

'Can I just be taking the little one?' she asked. I hung on to Eileen with both hands and began wailing. The kindly woman patted me on the head. She turned to the walrus-man and laughed.

'Well now, it looks like I'll be taking the two of them then, and I hope that's all right,' she said.

'Right madam,' he replied, a look of relief spreading over his face. He wrote something in a book, handed her some papers and off we went, just like that. We were going to live with strangers, who talked as though they were singing. It was difficult to understand what they were saying, but what ever it was, it sounded friendly...

DOROTHY PURDEW

Dorothy is the co-owner of Champneys with her son Stephen. This is extracted from a book about Henlow Grange, one of the resorts. It is partly written from the third person and also in the first.

Dorothy's journey to Henlow started back in the 1960s when she decided to lose weight. 'I went to Weight Watchers in a small village hall near Guildford. I lost weight although I did it through the diet my doctor had given me: Weight Watchers gave me the company and the incentive. But after I'd got down to eight and a half stone, I couldn't help thinking that I could run a class as well. So afterwards, I applied. I wore a smart pink suede coat – well, you would dress smartly if you were going to an interview, wouldn't you? – and borrowed my husband's flash car. The interviewer asked me how much money my husband earned and I told her I didn't think it was relevant. She then told me that I wouldn't earn very much working for Weight Watchers so she didn't know if it was worth me applying!'

Never one to be daunted, Dorothy decided to set up her own slimming clubs. 'In fact, it was the doctor who had drawn up the diet who gave me the idea. He said I could use the same diet so I hired a hall and got four people and those four brought some more and it spread. Everyone went to the loo

before weighing themselves but the loo was ⟨
the dark so they went in pairs with a torc
fantastic; he'd go round and distribute ac
through front doors.'

The slimming clubs got so successful that they spread witᵤ.
the area. Sometimes, Dorothy would invite some of the
women home for a few days in order to help them. As she
says 'When you're in someone else's house, it's not so easy to
raid the fridge'.

It was a perfect recipe except that, as Dorothy's husband
pointed out, it could go further. 'If you're going to put these
women up like a health farm, free of charge, you might as
well charge them for it,' he said. So the Purdews set about
finding a suitable house to do this – even though they didn't
have a budget for the kind of big place which would suit these
needs.

Then one day in 1978, an estate agent rang up Dorothy and
told her about an incredible house in Northampton, which
was going virtually free. Surely there had to be a catch? There
was. Apparently, the home had belonged to an elderly man
who had, when young, been in love with the same woman
that his brother had been in love with. The woman had
married the other man but the two brothers had stayed
friends and the one who died left his house to his brother's
grandson who was only 17 and too young to move in. 'So the
family was looking for someone who would live there and be
responsible for all the repairs,' recalls Dorothy. 'It seemed
perfect! We spent our savings on equipment and began my
first health farm.'

At first it seemed like a gift horse. Dorothy had her 'perfect'
house and clients immediately signed up. Stephen, who'd
always been supportive of his mother's dream, would serve
breakfast before going off to college. But within months, it
was clear there was a problem. For a start, the house could
only take 20 guests and the continual repairs on the house
drained the Purdews' resources. Within three years, it became
clear that they couldn't carry on even though Bob was

working and Dorothy had her income from the slimming clubs.

The Purdews then heard that Henlow Grange was for sale. 'My husband kept saying "But we can't afford it" and I knew he was right. But I dragged him along "just to have a look" and as soon as we drove down the drive, I fell in love with it. It was a lovely June morning and all the roses were out in full bloom. Immediately I knew I wanted to buy it.'

But the owner wanted £3million which was impossible even in Dorothy's dreams, so she reluctantly put her imagination away and carried on with the business. 'Then two years later in 1981, the estate agent rang and suggested we went round once more. By then, the property market was doing odd things and some houses were going for a song. I went on my own this time and the owner asked how much I would pay for the house. I plucked a figure out of the air – £350,000 – and she nearly bit my hand off in accepting it!'

Later, Dorothy describes her first night at Henlow.

'My husband was working so I was left on my own for the first night! I'll never forget that evening: there were two male guests and one woman and I was the only one there to man the bar. By 1.30am, they still hadn't gone home and I was thinking "What have I done?". Then one of the men went off to bed with the woman and the other man turned to me and made a suggestion. I spent the next half hour trying to escape him – which I did – but when I woke up the morning all on my own in this huge house, I did feel more than a twinge of unease... When I told Bob and Stephen, they immediately closed the bar until we got new staff!

'The first thing we did was to hire teams of cleaners from the village and asked them to work in pairs. Each one had their own designated area in the house so they took pride in cleaning it.' It was clever psychology...

Not wanting to lose a minute, Dorothy started trading as a health resort immediately. She and Bob sold the family home and soon they were all living together in two small bedrooms at the top of the house.

'Money was tight and I still had to pay the bailiff off weekly from the previous health farm. But I had a good relationship with him – once when we were out shopping, Bob and I bumped into him and we exchanged pleasantries. Bob said "You've done well if the bailiff is your new best friend!"

'We only just about got by because Bob was working and I still had my slimming clubs. I remember one night when I was really upset about it all because we were broke and I broke down. "I'm really sorry for spending all our money," I sobbed to Bob but he just told me not to stop crying. "No one's died," he said and that put it into perspective.

'It took about two years to put Henlow on its feet. Stephen was a fantastically hard worker; Bob was working hard too and as I said, I also had my slimming clubs. Every penny we had went back into the business.'

The recipe was beginning to work. But then tragedy stepped in. Ironically, given Bob's earlier remark about death, he developed lung cancer and died very suddenly in 1990.

It isn't a time Dorothy wants to dwell on but it was a tough period in her life – and one which she couldn't have got through without her son Stephen. Within a year, they bought Springs and then Forest Mere (1996); Inglewood (1998) and Champneys in Tring in 2000.

Later, Dorothy describes how she found out she'd been awarded an OBE in 2008 in recognition of her services to the spa industry.

'The news that I got it came completely out of the blue. I was dashing off to the airport earlier this year, when a phone call came and I nearly didn't take it. But then the caller said she was from the Cabinet Office. Apparently, they'd sent two letters which I don't recall and they wanted to know if I was offered an OBE, would I accept it.

'I thought it was a wind up but I said yes anyway. Then she faxed through a plain sheet of A4 asking me to give details like name and address and ethnic origin, etc. To be honest, I didn't think any more of it until June when I got another form but still no one said I definitely had the OBE! I was told that the newspapers might ring me just before the list came out in the summer but as they didn't contact me, I presumed I didn't have it.

'I always look up the honours on the net when they come out as a friend of the family has been hoping for one for years. As I scrolled down, my name jumped out at me! I couldn't believe it. In fact, I felt completely shocked. So I texted Stephen who was in a nightclub in Greece and he said "I'm coming back tomorrow."

'Meeting the Queen was a very unreal experience. She was much smaller than I thought and she said "I believe you have been given the OBE for your services to the spa industry". I said "Yes, ma'am". But then I don't know what she said next because I was so busy concentrating on going backwards without falling! Afterwards, we had a small family celebration at a restaurant in Windsor and then a party for friends and staff. It was wonderful.'

MARGARET (68)

You don't have to be famous to write your life story. Margaret came to me for help in writing hers because, like so many others, she wanted to leave a 'time capsule' behind. She also needed a project after being widowed. This is how her life story opened: as you will see, nothing dramatic happens but it is a lovely, gentle account of life in England during the 1930s. Margaret chose to write her story under general headings instead of referring to specific dates.

My parents' background

My mother was called May Grace Lewis and was one of five children: Ina, the twins Vincent and Vera (who died at 28 from a blood clot) and Reginald. May had to get a job at 16 because her parents Agnes, who was Scottish, and Ernest had separated and her mother needed the money. For married couples to separate in those days was a serious social stigma and my mother took the humiliation very badly, blaming her father for many years. Only later did she find out that her mother had probably had a relationship with someone else, so there were faults on both sides. Ina was the only one who kept in touch with her father, which says a good deal about her because she was a kind person.

May applied for the job of office assistant to the firm of FJ and JT Black, a new tailoring business. Although she didn't know it at the time, her boss, Frederick James Black, was to be her future husband and my father. However, it wasn't love at first sight. He was eight years older at the time and she was a pretty and flirtatious young lady who probably had several admirers at church and its badminton club which was the pivot of social life in those days.

Over time, a relationship must have occurred with her boss and they married on June 10th 1934 when she was 21 and he was 28. My mother then gave up work because that was what happened in those days.

My father had been born in 1904 and was brought up on a farm in Kirkcudbrightshire in Scotland along with his brothers and sister Samuel, Joseph, Bob, John (who died aged one from acute kidney disease) and Dora who also died at the age of one from gastroenteritis. No one seems to know how and it was never spoken about. In those days, there were no antibiotics which was why so many babies and children died. My father was only five when Dora died but he never talked about her to us. Perhaps that's why he adored me and my sister because we were his 'precious girls'.

During the early '20s, agriculture in Scotland was not going through a good patch and times were hard. My father's cousin Joseph Carson was in business in Birkenhead and knowing how the family in Scotland were struggling, he sent for my father's brother Joe to come and serve an apprenticeship with him in his 'credit' drapery business. This meant people could order suits without having to pay for them in full at the time. It's similar to credit today but was very new in those days when few working class people had bank accounts. So credit, where the customer would pay a set amount each week, was helpful providing it was kept in check. It's interesting to know how this worked: each customer would have a page in a ledger and all the accounts had to be entered by hand. My mother did most of this although I did too, as I got older. I actually enjoyed it because ledgers were kept so neatly. All calculations were done without the aid of a calculator.

Shortly afterwards, my father Frederick was also sent for to serve his apprenticeship. He was 19 at the time and described by Belle, Joseph's daughter and a second cousin of mine, as having a rosy complexion and black curly hair. My father and his brother lived with the Carsons over the business in Cole Street, Birkenhead and Belle recalls happy times such as playing draughts, card games, listening to the gramophone and taking Pip the dog for long walks. There was no tv or radio in the house! Once, my father and brother returned to Scotland on their motorbike to visit their parents and found Pip had followed them onto the ferry which crosses the Mersey. Rather than bringing him back, they took him on their motorbike all the way there!

Eventually Joe and Fred opened their own credit drapery business also in Cole Street and it was then that my mother went to work for them. (There was no rivalry; in fact it ended up with three shops owned by different members of the family in the same street.) According to my second cousin Belle, my father was struck by her from the moment she joined but knew he had to wait until she got older.

Even though I always thought my father was a quiet man, he had an outgoing personality which he passed down to Ian, my older brother. He was a hard worker and very fashionable: when spats were in fashion, he wore them with great aplomb and he never went without his Trilby hat. (Spats were a trouser decoration which slipped over the shoe and up the leg.)

My early childhood

I was born at 8.15pm on April 12th in 1940 and grew up in Glenavon Road, Birkenhead, Cheshire with two older brothers and a twin sister. My brothers are called Ian and Graham and my twin sister is Rosemary. We're not identical. We were close because she was born with severely impaired eyesight – the results of too much oxygen at birth. We were both six weeks premature but Rosemary only weighed three pounds and I was a big bouncing baby.

My mother didn't even know she was having twins: I was the second. I grew up knowing this as my mother told friends many times, I was a complete and utter shock! We were christened immediately in the nursing home where we were born because my sister's life was in the balance. I became Margaret Craik and my sister Rosemary Tait; our middle names being our grandmothers' maiden names. Neither of us liked our middle names as children but now we do because they are a family record.

I later found out that Rosemary had been born with a cowl over her face. It's like a very fine netting that is part of the membrane. Apparently it means you will never drown. My mother kept it in an envelope and we found it when she died last year.

My earliest memories are of always making sure I held Rosemary's hand wherever we went. Life was never dull! I became my sister's second pair of eyes – a role I took to easily because I loved her so much. But on occasions when I wasn't looking, she did things like walk into lamp posts and when she broke her collar bone and her knee cap, not to mention gashing her forehead, it was my fault. I never thought 'poor me'. It was my job and I was happy to do it.

We had a full time nanny and a housekeeper so had a privileged childhood even though we grew up during the war. One important adult in my life was my mother's sister Ina: she was very different from May because she was fun and outgoing and didn't worry about her appearance. It didn't concern her if things didn't match but my mother needed to make sure everything did. In those days, people had nicely permed hair but hers was naturally untidy in a nice way. She giggled a lot and I think that's what I liked about her because there wasn't a lot of giggling in our house. She was married and had four children but we didn't see much of them until they moved to Llandudno and then we saw more of them. We had lots of other cousins living near us as well, from both sides of the family.

It must have been difficult for our parents, bringing up children during the war. My father took an allotment as part of the 'Dig For Victory' campaign when everyone was encouraged to use every available piece of land to grow vegetables. I can still remember carrying cabbages back into the house. He also kept hens and I remember my parents talking about them being broody although I never understood what that meant. I would feed them: they had names and although it sounds awful, I recall eating Polly! It seemed quite natural at the time. There was a great community spirit and neighbours would share their fresh vegetables.

When I was two, the house was bombed. I don't remember that: we had an air raid shelter in the garden and the story goes that everybody went into the air raid shelter but because my sister and I were asleep, we were put under the kitchen table, wrapped in blankets. No one was with us. My eldest brother Ian was very distressed because he couldn't understand why we were left on our own. The air raid shelter was fitted out with camp beds, a paraffin stove and a small electric light bulb. There were no windows.

Perhaps my parents wondered if they'd done the right thing when they got into that air raid shelter but they couldn't go back to get us as there was a total blackout and people had to pay heavy fines if an air-raid warden spotted so much as a chink of light, even from a torch. It should be remembered that Liverpool was the second largest port at the time.

I don't remember anything but my mother must have been distraught when she came out of the shelter and found the house had been hit. Luckily we were all right. However, because Birkenhead was being so badly bombed (it had an important shipyard Cammel Lairds and was close to Liverpool), my parents were very worried about our safety because it was a prime target for air raids, just as London was.

Towards the end of 1940, my father decided we should be voluntarily evacuated to relatives on a farm in Castle Douglas in Scotland. Ian was the only one old enough to go to school but it was very hard for him. At the age of five, he had to travel on the local bus into Kirkcudbright, stay for lunch with an elderly lady who lived next to the school (later he recalled her as being austere with hair scraped back into a bun) and return in the afternoon to the farm. Poor Ian found it hard to fit in with the other children: he couldn't understand their Scottish accents and they bullied him because of his English accent. He found himself caught up in many fights and developed a stammer, probably due to his difficult time at school. Fortunately he grew out of it. My mother often spoke about the cold winter there – remember, there wasn't any central heating in those days!

My father wanted us nearer so in 1942, my father managed to rent a holiday home in Prestatyn. He couldn't go because he had to stay at home for the business. He also did Home Guard duties as he didn't pass the medical to be called up. I think his heart was a problem because he'd had rheumatic fever as a child. We didn't realise until much later that the war was to take a terrible toll on our father's health. He worked tremendously long hours, as everyone did in those days because all the young men had been called up so it was impossible to get staff.

My father had a Ford car which had to be started with a heavy starting handle which wasn't ideal for his heart condition. However, he was lucky to have a petrol allowance because he was in the Home Guard as petrol rationing started in 1939. This meant that everyone was only allowed to buy so much a week so there would be enough oil for aircraft.

By now, Joe had died from a heart attack at 39 (heart disease ran in the family) so we went to Prestatyn with Joe and

Grace's children, Keith and Elspeth, who were my cousins but are now both dead. Grace stayed to help with the business so my mother had six children to look after although my father found her a maid called Clarice to help. When I look at the pictures on the beach, we all looked so happy! It was a summer of clear blue skies and sunshine but this was how I saw it, through the eyes of a child. For adults, it was undoubtedly a very frightening time. We were only in Prestatyn for six weeks because something happened to my brother Ian. It could have been fatal and it went like this.

One day at school, he was being bullied so badly by one particular boy that he ran out of the school with the other boy chasing him. Ian was so scared that he ran out into the road, straight in front of a grocery van. To everyone's amazement, he came crawling out from underneath – causing more shock to the driver than himself.

The story goes that the driver took him home. My mother called the doctor but amazingly, he was only suffering from shock. Nothing was broken but we moved back home shortly afterwards, possibly because of Ian's problems at school.

Back home again

When we got home, Clarice, the maid, went off to work on the land. In those days, women did a lot of agricultural work because men were away fighting. They also worked in factories which gave them a great deal of independence which lasted after the war. Some women must have resented giving this up (as well as their jobs) after the war. There were also tales of marriages breaking up and also of women remaining spinsters because their men never came back.

Clarice was replaced by Helen whom I liked very much. We went back to a bigger house two doors down the road: my brother Graham thinks we did an exchange with the neighbours who wanted to downsize. Our new house was 10 Prenton Hall Road, a very impressive corner plot with wonderful views over the Welsh hills and a large pond in the garden.

This turned out to be very significant. When my sister was about four or five, she fell in the pond – although it was big, she didn't see the edge. Fortunately, Graham was there and hung onto her by her hair while I ran into the house, screaming for help. I can still hear myself screaming and it sends shivers down my spine to remember it. I blamed myself for not being there to protect her.

At the new house, we had a wonderful next door neighbour whom we called 'Auntie'. We would often pop round there for delicious cakes and tea on the understanding that one of us brushed her hair! She was a bit older than our mother and was a lovely person. As we got older, she would take us to the cinema. In those days, everyone stood up to sing the National Anthem before the film started. The big treat was when she would buy us ice cream at the interval.

We all played war games and somehow my brothers had acquired German war helmets. I also remember clearly the boys coming back with part of a plane. They were very pleased but my mother was horrified. When I look back on the war, I don't recall feeling scared but I do remember the fun we had, playing in the fields or cycling on our bikes. My sister and I were usually on the back of our brothers' bikes and we all hung on for grim death! I remember one day getting my foot stuck in the spokes. Boys and girls all had fun together – a freedom that very few children still have today. If the girls were all playing together, we would play skipping games or hide and seek. The skipping games were 'Teddy bear, teddy bear, turn around' and 'Altogether girls, never mind the weather, girls...'

Nevertheless, signs of the war were never far away. There were large silver barrage balloons still floating in the sky waiting to catch low-flying enemy aircraft in the steel cables. One day in 1946, when my brothers were playing in the garden, they heard an explosion and saw plumes of black smoke in the distance. My mother didn't want Graham to go and look but Ian and my cousin Keith, who were playing with them at the time, were allowed to go and shot over on their bikes. Later, Ian confessed that curiosity made him go and see if the American pilot had a wristwatch. At the time, very few people in Britain had a watch because they still had fobs. It sounds awful but you need to see it from a child's point of view; war could seem exciting if you didn't fully understand what was going on.

To my father's horror, the boys brought back part of a door which he promptly turned over to the police. Apparently, it belonged to one of two American planes which had collided and crashed as they were approaching their base near Warrington. Later, we found out that both pilots had died. I don't remember this – especially as newspapers weren't allowed to report such things in case it helped the enemy – but unfortunately there were several incidents like that which occurred during the war.

ANGIE SPENDLOVE (LATE 50s)

Angie also came to me for help in writing her life story. She had quite a troubled complicated childhood and felt it might help to put it down on paper. There is, however, a great deal of humour which helps to lighten her story. She has chosen to tell it in chronological order, using general headings such as 'The early years', below. She also chose to refer to herself by another name 'Phoebe' to distance herself from what is quite a dramatic tale describing how Angie was adopted at the age of eight by her real parents who'd been unable to marry when she was born as her father was married to someone else. Angie also included quite a lot of dialogue and also letters so that her life story, at times, seems like a piece of fiction. This isn't always to everyone's taste but it does make the reader feel present at the time, so making the life story seem even more realistic. Angie is keen to find a publisher or agent for her life story which she has now completed.

The early years

My earliest memories of my life start here. The convent, previously a manor house, was medium size with spacious, light dormitories. Mine was on the ground floor and I shared this with nine other girls, aged between five and seven. One of the nuns slept in a private cubicle at the end, to keep an eye on us.

At the time there were about 60 boarders, making it small enough to be friendly. I was put in the charge of two senior girls and I can remember them taking it in turns to dress me and take me to the refectory where I would eat with other children, on the 'baby' table. We all had a tuck-box, and these were kept in cupboards at the end of the refectory with our names on. Some had cakes, but mine usually contained a small amount of sweets and a bottle of Virol, a spoonful of which I was given at tea-time every day.

Most days, I joined the kindergarten class for reading, writing and adding up. I still have my first end of term report which read: 'Phoebe is quite bright and shows intelligence, but talks too much in class!'

In between lessons and a short rest in the afternoons, I would accompany the gardener with a view to *helping!* However, I generally played with earth and water, making mud pies in the old terracotta flower pots.

I'd never been ill, until I went down with the dreaded attack of measles. Then I pined inconsolably for my mother. In a darkened room on my own, the isolation (apart from Teddy) was terrifying and although I had plenty of attention from the 'Infirmarian', she didn't take the place of Mother, so I scratched and cried a lot.

Mother came to see me once, but after she'd gone, I upset myself that she didn't come again until I was better, which seemed a very long time.

At weekends, we would go out. Not far. We spent a lot of time in the meadow where I was happy making daisy-chains and picking buttercups; the shiny yellow head would be put under my chin, always prompting the same reaction of delight when it was affirmed I liked butter!

Sometimes I would be taken back to Mrs Roberts' house. I enjoyed those trips, but, according to Mother, I got so upset at returning to school that it was hardly worth it. I don't know how long I stayed – it could have been for a weekend, a week, or even a day. Time didn't have any significance; only when I was waiting for a visit from Mother, ice-cream or sweets.

The summer, with the sweet smell of roses and freshly cut grass, meandered by, followed by autumn, when a curiously formal letter arrived from Daddy! I'd obviously met him before, on a couple, or maybe more, occasions. I was familiar with frequent affectionate letters from Mother. But Daddy? Sister Clara read it to me:

My dear Phoebe
I was with Mummy last Saturday and Sunday and have given her a few sweets for you, so don't forget to look very hard for them when Mummy writes next. I know how you look forward to her letters, but this time it will be a small parcel!

Mummy will not be able to come and see you for a little while, because she's very busy earning all those pennies so that you'll both be able to come and live with me.

I was hoping to have you both with me in London soon, but although you are still coming, you will have to wait a little while longer before we can all be together. Probably about the same time as Father Christmas comes along. However, I know you are very happy with the nuns, and sure you'll hardly notice the wait.

Now don't forget to be a good little girl, and as soon as I can, I will come down and see you.

God Bless You

Daddy.

Who was he? Why did I have a Daddy? Might this mean I wouldn't have a Mummy any more? Where was London? Sister Clara did her best to explain, but I don't think I really took it in. I had only ever had a Mummy, but I soon learnt from other children that they *all* had a Mummy and a Daddy.

I later found out that Mother's life had become intolerable since word had got around about her position. People were unwilling to accept such a situation, ignoring her in the street.

Some even called her names, and referred to me as a bastard. To make it worse, her money was dwindling with the strain of paying the fees, rent and the loan from Helen and Dick.

All this, left her with no other choice than to find my father [Joe]. Once again, they arranged to meet at Paddington Station. Finally conceding that without Joe in her life, who was conveniently now a widower, she asked him to marry her (mainly to 'give me a name'.) She would have to make the final sacrifice, and live with the man she abhorred.

Naturally I knew nothing of this arrangement. But more letters arrived from Daddy, in similar vein to the one below, written in 1950 on a Tuesday (no date), from London SW1:

Dear Phoebe

I want Mummy to read this little letter to you. You promised Daddy when I left you on Sunday that you would be a very good girl, so that we could all have a lovely time this weekend. But you haven't been good, have you?

How are we ever going to save up all our pennies so that you can come away with us both to Bournemouth if you are not a good girl? I shall not help you Phoebe dear unless you do as we tell you.

I won't be cross with you this time – so now you give Mummy a big kiss and tell her you won't be naughty – but try and always be a good girl. I shall ask you whether you have been when I see you on Friday.

So, good bye little girl – and try to be a nice little girl that Daddy will be proud of. You can if you like – can't you?

My love and a kiss for my small daughter.

Daddy x

* * *

By the time I was five, I don't know if I had been a good girl or not but they had got married! I didn't go to the actual ceremony but on the big day was looked after by Aunty Ada and Uncle Harry. They weren't relatives but what was the difference anyway? For the reception, I wore a beautiful taffeta, multi-colour striped, smocked, dress with a lovely sash tied in a bow at the back. It must surely have been a Harvey Nichols purchase!

There were many plates of very nice food, including cream cakes, ice-cream and jelly. Lots of people arrived at the house to celebrate, and I got a lot of attention.

My parents had cooked up a plausible story for the guests, neighbours and any future enquirers – Father had known Mother for years, and they had kept up their friendship since before the war. Mother's first husband, who was meant to be my original father and who was 'a great friend of theirs', had been killed in Dunkirk. After my father's wife died, they had become closer, consoling each other over their individual losses, and eventually fell in love. . .

The story for me to ingest was that Mummy and Daddy had prayed every night to have me; that I was very precious and they had waited so long to have me, omitting any information about my dead father. An element of the distorted truth remained for years to come.

The next recollections are more vivid, but as with all distant memories, bits are missing. I felt sick almost all of the time becoming extremely nervous (labelled, highly strung). This appeared to cause much anxiety between my parents, and the relentless rows that ensued made me feel worse.

We continued to live the lie after moving to the house in London with its latticed windows and shiny black painted front door. The house was comfortable and well equipped. We had a built in kitchen, which fascinated me, particularly the ironing board, which was hidden by a cupboard door. When opened, the ironing board folded out!

My bedroom with its dainty flowered pale pink wall-paper was pretty. It had matching curtains and bedspread, a darker pink carpet, and some pretty furniture which included a kidney shaped dressing-table.

Over time I became aware that all but a few of the contents of our home had been shared with someone else. Endless efforts on my mother's part were made to put away various ornaments and pictures, resulting in major scenes.

It was horrible! Father always blamed Mother for starting the row and he would shout while Mother wept. 'Be quiet. The neighbours will hear you!' she would weep. But he took no notice of her pleas, shouting all the louder.

There were a few happy times, in this already rocky marriage. There were visits to the zoo; the park (where my father taught me to row); occasional trips into the West End when we would visit Buckingham Palace to watch Changing the Guard; Trafalgar Square to feed the pigeons; Piccadilly Circus to admire the statue of Eros and some trips to Hamleys toy store.

However, all these prospective outings were measured by the weather. If there was enough blue sky to make a sailor's suit, we would go, but any threat of inclement weather and the trip would be cancelled, causing me huge disappointment, inevitably followed by tears! This reaction didn't go down well, and I was often not only sent to my bedroom, but locked in, making me cry all the more. Eventually a rash would appear on my forehead, the sight of which frightened me. Measles again? Mother used to say that if I didn't stop crying, the nasty rash would stay with forever, and any chance of remaining pretty, gone; and that would be my fault.

* * *

Mrs Waterhouse, a social worker, became quite a feature in our lives. She generally visited on a Saturday, and always wore a tweed skirt, which irritated my legs, when she asked me to sit on her lap. She was a kindly person, whom I called Aunty. Dressed in my best clothes, I would be encouraged to go out to play, on the premise that I should not get dirty, and to keep my socks and shoes clean. This often caused me a bit of bother, since going out to play meant riding my tricycle which often left black grease marks from the chain on my socks!

In the meantime, Mrs Waterhouse would have arrived and then the grown-ups would sit and talk for a while. Later I would be called in to join them. I deduced her visits carried a deal of importance, for before she arrived, Mother would clean the house from top to bottom and bake cakes!

When I was sitting on Mrs Waterhouse's knee, she always asked me questions, mostly about happiness. Did I like playing, reading, had I made any friends, and then (more darkly), was I happy with Mummy and Daddy in our new home? I answered positively to all these questions, since I was being trained from an early age not to talk about anything 'private' – this meant the rows!

I clearly played out my part admirably, for about ten months later, immaculately dressed, as were my parents, we went on a surprise outing. It rained, but this outing wasn't cancelled, so I guessed it must be very special. I was excited.

We arrived at a large, ornate building with a swathe of steps up to the entrance: the Town Hall. It smelt of a public place, sort of musty and disinfected, and made me feel sick. The shiny brown linoleum floors covered long corridors, with occasional clutches of utility chairs lined up like soldiers. We eventually found the right 'room'. Various official-looking people spoke with my parents, while we sat in the stark waiting area. I was very frightened, constantly asking if we could leave because I didn't like it. 'It won't be long and then we can all go home.'

Home? But we were supposed to be on a surprise outing! Was this it? Fear turned into disappointment, and tears fell down my face – a reaction my parents clearly didn't want. Not one bit! They desperately tried to console me with the promise of tea at Lyons Corner House at Marble Arch. That ensured I became dry eyed and smiling just in time to be called into another room. But what were we doing in church?

The court room was set out with desks, at which men and women sat bolt upright with batches of papers neatly laid out in front of them. One man was sitting on the stage! Various people including my parents, were called to a box. It was all rather boring. Sitting on a bench, swinging my legs I paid a lot of attention to Teddy until the man on the stage banged his desk with a hammer and we all stood up. Was he cross? We always took great care of our furniture. That hammer blow sealed my official adoption by my biological parents, and with the sweep of a pen, the name of McLeod was disbanded. My parents' relief was evident.

Once outside, we didn't go to the Corner House for tea, but straight home, changed into more casual clothes and listened to the Nuns Chorus, normally a Sunday pastime, on the gramophone.

After that, Mrs Waterhouse, with her scratchy skirts, mysteriously disappeared from our lives.

BEATRICE ELLIS
Beatrice came to me for help in writing her life story because she had 'reached the age where I want to write it all down'. She chose to take random sections of her life such as the one below:

A phase in my life

It was the early sixties, and it seemed that the entire country was wearing flowers in their hair, jumping and shouting to The Beatles, and generally having a high old time, except in Cornwall. This was not the San Francisco of the West Country. Especially my little town tucked right down in the boot, St Ives. Loved by artists and holiday makers, the residents struggled to survive, having fun and dancing was not high on their agenda, unless you went to the local pubs.

I was 15, a dangerous age for a girl in this culture, particularly for one that had been brought up in a first class hotel. The hotel and its visitors would give me messages of 'things can be better than this' but as a 'girl beneath the stairs', how could this be achieved?

I was an only child, my parents worked the expected hours of hoteliers; which, during the season, were 24/7. They were lucky, in a way, that I spent considerable time in the local hospital as a patient with chronic asthma. The hospital became the place I felt I belonged. So, when leaving school it was the career I would choose. I could have gone to Penzance, 20 miles away, to train in the large hospital there, but in the early 60s it was hardly the height of hedonism.

I applied to train in some of the training hospitals further up the country, in larger cities. Dudley Road Hospital in Birmingham accepted me just on the references given by the matron at the hospital where I was now working as an 'assistant'. In the backwater of my Cornish town I had received a poor formal education, not helped by lack of schooling during my time in hospital, nevertheless, I was in, and so excited to be leaving Cornwall, I felt I had found freedom, I had in fact escaped.

The end of the summer season in Cornwall is an anti-climax. The weather cools, the autumn sun goes pale, and the drizzle gets cold. Although during the summer, the 'groccles' are a painful thorn in the locals' side, they are, at first missed, just for their sheer volume, noise and colour.

For me it was wonderful, a constant reminder that I was leaving. At a loose end some evenings, I would go with a friend to have a drink at a cocktail bar in a local hotel. The bar man Tommy would serve us the requested Brandy and Babyshams at a quarter of the price. This evening we were giggling about things 15 and 16 years old giggle about, when the most gorgeous young man sprang down the steps into the bar. Tall, and dressed elegantly in smart casuals, he had blonde curls, blue eyes and the loveliest smile showing beautiful straight, white teeth I had ever seen.

Now, although it could be argued, on a night out at the end of the season, even the seagulls looked attractive, but this guy was. I looked and wanted. He came over to the bar and said in the broadest Birmingham accent I had ever heard 'Now then girls, what would you like to drink?' My friend seemed unable to answer, so I did for the both of us, scared of missing an opportunity or of letting him go. 'Two Brandy and Babyshams please.' He barely concealed a look of horror and said 'What do you follow that with love, a shot of paraffin?' I smiled and said 'No, I usually follow it with another, thank you.' He flashed me his beautiful grin, and ordered.

DEBORAH TRENCHARD
Deborah is a self-published author who has had a varied life. After growing up in Barbados, she went to New York and then on to England. The following is an extract from her book Finding Me*.*
Finding Me: a Life in transition, Deborah Trenchard (Author House, 2007)

It was a Sunday, mid-April. I left Barbados filled with excitement and fervour for a two-week holiday in New York. I arrived at JFK late afternoon. I stepped off the plane fashioned in a see-through blouse, a mini skirt, and six-inch heels! I was greeted by a sea of people in the arrivals hall. I looked for my relatives. Then I spotted my grandmother, Linda, my older sister, and my Uncle Peter on the balcony above. They waved. My maternal grandmother, Elise, had been living in New York since the mid-sixties. It was she who had sent me a 'letter of invitation', the prerequisite for obtaining a visa to enter the United States. I looked across the heaving airport hall wondering where my relatives had disappeared to. I followed a crowd of people through the exit door, but was immediately shocked by freezing air. I placed my luggage on the ground and wrapped my arms tightly around my body in a frantic attempt to protect myself from this howling wind. My teeth chattered, my breath froze, my fingers and feet, numb; my shoes now two sizes too small. My running nose, well! I swayed my caressed body gently. I watched as passengers queued for taxis. I kept my eyes open in all directions looking for my relations. I checked the time. Fifteen minutes gone. It felt like hours. Stiff as a corpse, I waited. One middle-aged lady, dressed enviably warmly in her heavy fur coat, hat and gloves, gave me a questioning look. She asked if I was okay. 'I hope you find your family soon,' she said and headed off. Then I heard a voice from behind say, 'What happened? How did you get here?' It was my sister Linda, with a warm coat! 'We've been looking around the hall for you. Gran is worried sick.' I couldn't speak. Although I tried to; all one could hear was the sound of chattering teeth.

The sight of this long, wide, luminous bridge we were crossing was amazingly spectacular. I wondered if New York was real, or was it just an incredible Hollywood film set. The Triboro Bridge made the tiny bridge in Bridgetown look insignificant.

'That building you can see over there in the distance, with the slender spire in the middle in green fluorescent lighting, is the Empire State Building,' Linda said.

'And what's the other building with the gold lights which look like. . .' I hesitated, 'crescents, I suppose.'

'That's the Chrysler Building,' my Uncle Peter said.

Childlike, my gazed flicked in wonderment. The bright lights; the different shaped buildings, the large boards advertising Pan American Airlines with its slogan 'makes the going great', Kool cigarettes, Land-o-Lakes butter, Dodge Cars. Mesmerising. There were other bridges to my left and right. Now over the bridge, my eyes flicked from shop windows to the large apartment blocks.

Uncle Peter decided to give me a short sightseeing tour of Manhattan. Park Avenue, wow! The place I'd seen in those black and white movies. Mind you, we'd only had television at home for a couple of years. So this movie watching was new. Still, from what I'd seen on the screen, the rich and famous lived on Park Avenue. And the doormen stood outside their buildings opening the doors like those we were passing. There was the Alfred Dunhill store displaying men's fashion. I'd never heard of Cartier and wasn't quite sure how to pronounce it!

'This street is so wide,' I said, to no one in particular.

'This is New York,' Linda piped in. 'All the streets are wide,' my sister said, knowingly.

I kept 'wowing'! The beautiful shoes, the glamorous handbags, oh! I wondered if I would be able to afford this lifestyle one day. As we drove, I dreamed.

'We're going to see Macy's,' Uncle Peter said.

'What's Macy's?' I felt silly.

'The world's largest department store,' Linda said.

'This is it here on the left,' Uncle Peter said.

My bottom lip dropped, making any wowing difficult to exit my mouth. My eyes bulged.

Linda indicated the full length of the sprawling store. Its window display caused me to drool. Surreal!

'Wow. This is all one store?' Bowled over I repeated, 'All one store?'

'Get out of the car and have a look,' Linda suggested.

Now slightly thawed, I stepped out of the car, eagerly, with childlike excitement.

This, I whispered, is one store! My head moved slowly up and down the majesty of this building, in awe. The outside world!

Driving off again, my Uncle Peter said, 'This is the famous Fifth Avenue'.

The movies, was all I could think of. Since leaving the airport my eyes and mouth remained in more or less the same position.

'Fifth Avenue,' I heard myself say.

There, stores called Lord and Taylor, B. Altman, and more.

I got out of the car again and looked skywards; it was possible that my neck had never before been in such a position. I felt small, insignificant. I looked up and down the bustling street: buses, taxis and cars, all honking their horns. It was a magical moment, and I didn't want it to end.

Reluctantly I got back into the car. Destination: Brooklyn.

Things changed dramatically though as we reached lower Manhattan. The expensive jewellery stores and manikins draped in beautiful couture were now conspicuous by their absence. The neighbourhoods got grottier as we crossed over the Brooklyn Bridge. There was very little by way of excitement en route to my grandmother's. We chitchatted as we drove. The usual: How are things back home? How is so-and-so doing? I told Linda, my older sister by one year, that her friend Maureen had sent her a package. I had no idea what its contents were. Linda had been living in New York for three years and had only returned to Barbados once.

'Hope your mother sent me some rum?' my uncle said.

Uncle Peter, a tall smooth-skin black man, remained quiet for the rest of the journey. He was my mother's older brother, and the pride and joy of his mother. Consequently, he couldn't put a foot wrong.

Uncle Peter left shortly after we arrived at my grandmother's apartment, cradling his bottle of Mount Gay rum.

The following morning I awoke to a note, or rather, to a lengthy diatribe, barely legible, that my grandmother had written, warning again of the hazards of New York, Brooklyn especially. She and Linda had gone off to work. A list of instructions on how to find my way around was left on the kitchen table. But it would be advisable to stay indoors! This note included the instruction – in the event that I got lost: 'PLEASE DO NOT ASK A STRANGER'. But who else was I supposed to ask? Both she and Linda left phone numbers where they could be contacted should the inevitable happen.

I wrapped my sister's thick robe tightly around my shivering body and walked to the back window. I was horrified by the sight of the derelict buildings across the way, nothing more than charred ruins. Peering through the net curtains I looked from left to right, but I could see nothing but dereliction. I closed my eyes in disbelief. What had happened to the New York I had seen the previous evening? Where was Park Avenue? I turned the radio on and sat in the kitchen listening to the news bulletins. There were reports of muggings, shootings, gang warfare and arson, to name but a few. My knees quaked. My heart pounded. I wondered how on earth I was going to survive, on my own, and on my first day, in what seemed to me like the 'battlefields' of Brooklyn. Sitting snugly in my thick robe, sipping a cup of tea, I picked up my grandmother's note again and tried to digest her instructions. My first thought was to go for a walk, if only as far as the next street, the corner, stand on the step, anything.

I looked at the clock, hanging somewhat lopsidedly on the wall. It was nearly ten-thirty. My throat was a bit sore. Thankfully my body hadn't responded more severely to my stint outside the airport. I scanned the kitchen. It was a large room with a high ceiling and brownish yellow paint peeling off in places. A wire shopping cart stood on the floor, stuffed with brown paper bags and various pieces of junk. My grandmother had always hoarded, from what I could remember of her in Barbados. An assortment of wall plaques hung on the wall: 'Home Sweet Home', 'God Bless Our Home', and a badly chipped spoon in the shape of a pineapple with the word BARBADOS splashed across it. I walked over to the well-stocked Armada refrigerator that stood majestically against one wall. I opened the door, and was overwhelmed. Before my eyes stood giant tubs of ice cream in a variety of flavours, huge buckets of chicken, an enormous carton of orange juice, a gallon bottle of apple juice and much, much, more. I stood mesmerised, holding the door open, looking at this mound of food as one would a fine painting. I had bacon and eggs. I forgot to mention that there must have been about five packets of bacon on one shelf!

After I had breakfasted I decided to 'brave it'; go outside. Oh, the attire. One would have thought that I was off the Antarctica, bar the moon boots! They would have given me away, alerting everyone to the fact that I had just arrived from some part of the Caribbean. This was something my sister had mentioned the previous evening in the car. 'Don't, for goodness sakes, be too conspicuous. Try to act like everyone else.' She had also mentioned, numerous times, that I should watch my handbag. Very important. Crucial.

Linda had left me some of her warm, but oversized, clothing. So there I stood tucking my money away, here and there. I left the television on – my grandmother's orders – and carefully secured the numerous locks before leaving the apartment. Oh, and the chain lock as well! 'Always remember to put the chain on first!' This was after a short demonstration. Should a burglar fight his way through the other six or so locks, the chain would stop him from going any further! Surely. And the culprit could, according to my sister, be residing upstairs. 'You never know,' she said, as we snuggled down to sleep, she on one sofa and me on the put-you-up bed in the living room. Paranoid, I kept checking: putting each key back in its correct lock; unlocking and relocking – just to make sure, as I imagined a prison warden would. I had just arrived from one of the safest places in the world. Back home we closed our doors, but never locked them. The key lived over the door. I'd never carried a key until that moment.

Once outside I had to be vigilant.

Bravely, I stepped out into what were, according to the weatherman, unseasonably freezing temperatures. I turned right out of the apartment like someone who knew exactly where she was headed. At the end of the block I turned left. I proceeded to walk along Nostrand Avenue in Bedford-Stuyvesant. Bed Sty, for short! I was immediately shocked by what greeted me. I wanted to return to Barbados without delay. The shops looked dirty, uninviting. Some boarded up, others burnt to a cinder. Vagrants and winos hung out on the streets with their bottles in brown paper bags, from which they swigged as they swayed. On these insalubrious streets there was much standing around, flailing hands and what seemed to be arguments about any and everything that had, according to them, caused them to be in their current state: anything from politics to the Vietnam War. People spoke to each other in a manner that was somewhat foreign to me. For the first time I heard the phrases: 'you mother-f. . .ker', and, 'you f. . .ing black son-of-a-bitch', or, 'you say that to me one mo' goddam time and I'm gon' kick your f. . .ing black ass'. Though Caribbean men hung around and swore, equally, still, this language was new to me. The men in Barbados called each other, when arguing, 'shites' or 'raa. . .soles', and they also used the 'c' word a lot!

Meandering along the crowded street I turned right, looking for a shop that sold clothes. Ah, I spotted one. This store sold everything from clothes to pots and pans, and all on the same floor. I bought two sweaters, which I held up to my body in an attempt to judge whether they would fit. I asked the Spanish man behind the cash register if I would be able to return them if I needed to. 'Ya sure can,' he said, madly chewing gum.

I kept walking along Fulton Street for quite a considerable distance. The record shops belted out all kinds of music: jazz, R and B, the latest hits, mostly Motown. The Jackson Five's *ABC* was another favourite. But the most popular song seemed to be Freda Payne's *Bring the Boys Home. . .Bring them back alive.* I'd heard it on the radio at least three times since I awoke.

My eyes and ears were on full alert. Listening to conversations about things that hadn't been a part of my life in paradise: protest marches by black civil rights activists. There appeared to be a ground swell of anger and, from what I could gauge, blacks living in these ghettos seemed to be declaring war on themselves. The black civil rights movement was in full swing. Black Muslim men, with their close-cut hair, some wearing African dress, were selling tabloid newspapers at every corner. In spite of being in the middle of this frenetic activity, and supposedly dangerous streets, I felt a sense of 'safety'. My 'sightseeing' tour was continuously interrupted by the whirring noise of sirens from ambulances, fire engines and police cars. In Barbados I had only ever heard the fire brigade, never a police car.

STEPHEN (70)

I suggested to Stephen that he wrote his life story using the Desert Island Discs format as it was a shorter method than some of the others. Stephen has been used to writing in a more formal office style so this approach was less daunting because he only had to write five fairly brief accounts describing his life so far. Below is the first. To his surprise (and mine), Stephen revealed a slightly humorous, tongue-in-cheek tone as you will see.

First piece of music

I was born in a Yorkshire nursing home and apparently, the nurse who delivered me said that I would be Prime Minister one day! I don't know why she said that but my mother said I had a sort of authority about me.

I don't remember the birth, obviously, but I do know that it was five months before the start of the Second World War. I was not to know my father until I was about seven or eight. (More of which in the next section.) It transpired that he spent a long time in Italy in the RAF police alongside Eric and Abe Bedser, both cricketing legends. He could not have been near the front lines since he witnessed Gigli in *Tosca* and many operas in Naples and Rome and I only recently passed his collection of programmes and press cuttings to an opera enthusiast.

Realistically, the first thing I recall in any detail was being taken for a walk in my pram to a nearby hamlet to see where a bomb had landed, jettisoned from a German bomber, fleeing after a raid on Liverpool. Not for me, the London blitz, I was 240 miles north. I do remember the air raid sirens, the shelter and the blackouts. Not a glimmer of light should escape. Only gas provided light then and there were no motorways or street lit roads. We were in farming country.

We lived in a row of eight large three-storey
The nursing home was number one in the rov
was number five so my mother hadn't had f;
birth to me. My grandparents on my mother's
us. Grandpa, my surrogate dad, a veterar
trenches and the Royal Artillery of the First world war,
was then a police constable. On Sundays, he used to take me
to the pub called The King William IV (Billy), both during and
after the war. I would have a lemonade and would sit next to
him on a bench, dressed in my Sunday hat and coat. The room
was full, thick with smoke and the pianist would have all the
customers singing along 'Pack up Your Troubles'; 'Show Me
the Way to Go Home' and similar songs. The pub closed for
the day at 1.00pm.

In 1946, my father's sister Susan was married. She's still alive,
now 93. During the war, when she was a WAF, she lost a leg. I
don't know how that happened – I never dared ask her as a
child because it seemed too delicate a matter. Her wedding
reception was at the local pub and it was the first time I had
seen an iced cake with three tiers. They were both good cooks
and Edward, her husband, was a gem at cake decoration. One
strange irony was that my father and Dick knew each other
because they lived in the same village. But they didn't know
that they had both been in Rome during the war! Dick was in
the army and my father was in the air force and communica-
tion wasn't what it was like now.

Piece of music to recall this time
'I believe' sung by Frankie Laine. I'll never forget the lines:

'For every drop of rain that falls, a flower grows
Someone in the great somewhere, hears every word.'

Frankie Laine recorded it in 1953 but I know we had the sheet
music in the house before then. It got to number one in the
top of the charts.

Second piece of music
I was seven or eight when my father returned from the war. I
can remember him coming home. We went to meet him at the

railway station and mother saw him before the train actually stopped at the platform. He had his head out of the window. After that it was a bit of a haze but it seemed odd having him at home. It was another big body in the house and the rooms weren't very big. I was very close to my mother and I think I resented having him back. I can't remember doing much with him until the winter of 1947/8 when we had a big snow. He bought me a sledge – the type you push with your feet. I had a lot of fun with that for years. He showed me how it worked and that helped a bit. It might be difficult for people to understand today but the war divided people; my mother and my grandmother were the people I knew best.

One event which stands out in my mind was when I was about 12 in 1951. My aunts Nancy and Margaret spruced me up to take me on a train to Lancaster to see the King and Queen when they made their Royal Visit with Princess Margaret. I recall the princess wearing pink. My aunts had put Brylcreme on my hair – far too much it transpired – and plastered it down with a parting down the middle before jamming my school cap on top. Standing on the pavement outside the town hall in the sunshine, with thousands of other people, I suddenly became aware of something cold and wet trickling down my neck. The Brylcreme was pouring off! It became a family joke for years later! The King and Queen were in an open-topped saloon and Margaret sat in front. They weren't in full regalia and seemed very normal.

I got to know my father better when I was 15 or 16 and doing quite well at school. I was interested in sport and became house captain of athletics, cricket and fives. I played rugby for every school team. My father was proud of this and would come along and watch matches. He was also a good cricket player himself. By then he was working for a firm of lawyers (he rejoined the firm he'd worked for before as a probate clerk) and encouraged me to become a lawyer.

Music
The National Anthem played by a brass band. Whenever I hear the National Anthem, I think of this.

Third piece of music

I left school at 18 in 1957 and did five years' articles with the law firm at home. I enjoyed that and, during the articles, attended Manchester University. I lived at home which was what happened in those days. I joined a cricket and rugby club and that was part of my social life. At one stage, I played against the entire Yorkshire team.

I met my wife when I was about 20: she worked for a firm of accountants. The law firm I was working for had an office in the same town and I delivered letters so came across her that way. We also used to have Saturday night dances at the local hotel and we recognised each other. It was love at blushing first sight! We got married at the end of 1963, three years later, after I'd qualified.

We had our first rented house: six guineas a week, it cost. It was a two bedroom barn conversion and it was in the grounds of a larger house. My first car was an MGA salmon pink drop head coupe. Very sleek! The firm lent me the money to buy it and I repaid it every week. They thought the young aspiring lawyer should have an appropriate car! I thought I was the bee's knees.

Music

Bach's 'Toccata and Fugue'. This was played at our wedding. Magnificent!

MIKE'S FIRST CAR

Mike, 56, used the First method to write his life story after being pestered by his children to write down some of his memories. This is what he wrote under the section 'First Car'. You will see that just by thinking about his car, he remembered other things from that period, too.

My first car was a Mini in 1973. It was white with a black roof and cost £65. I bought it from a friend of my father and had it for a couple of years. At the time, I was a student reading economics at Nottingham. I remember a wonderful sense of freedom – I was a student AND I had a car of my own!

Ironically, this was considered the summer of discontent because of the miners' strike and the three day week. We had power strikes and petrol rationing was threatened. I still have the vouchers that were issued although we never had to use them.

At the time, I was living in a shared house which was very sparse in terms of furniture. Bare floor boards and no carpets. We wore flared jeans, had long hair and played Status Quo all the time!

KEITH'S FIRST CAR
Keith was born in India but has lived in England for many years. He wanted to write his life story to tell his children what it was like to come to this country. He linked this in with memories of his first car.

The first car that I drove was actually my father's Morris Minor in 1967 in India. I was very careful with it and didn't prang it! After school, I worked for a bank in England although would come back to India regularly. I bought a small Fiat in 1978 and although I loved it, I was rather embarrassed by the colour – turquoise! But it was the only car I could afford. It was actually stolen and then abandoned. Friends used to joke that the thief was too embarrassed to be seen with a turquoise car! It was one of my first experiences of England.

HILARY SKELTON'S STORY
Hilary was one of my students at a creative writing course and is currently writing her life story. She has kindly allowed me to use extracts from the period between 1944 and 1950. The extract provides a good example of how much you can cram in within a short period of time – and also how detail can make the story come to life.

Birth
My conception occurred, to the surprise and dismay of my parents, sometime during the beginning of August 1944. I made my appearance on the 11th April 1945, an Aries child,

full of fire and creativity, and powerful lungs, but according to my mother premature and with a puny physique. My survival, then, was a triumph, if not of medical intervention, then of my determination to BE someone.

Living with adults
The mysterious world of adulthood, with its many problems, became at once fascinating and frightening. On the radio there were such curious programmes as 'Currenty Vence'. What on earth was currenty vence? I imagined a kind of steamed pudding, a cook, metal pudding moulds, currants, or perhaps sultanas. The content of the programme escaped me. Prime minister meant nothing. Budget, rationing, troops, and that stirring music that seemed to be on the radio most of the time were meaningless, but somehow created an atmosphere, grave and alarming in the back room. My impression of the adult world became one of vague and unspoken threat, secrets, disapproval and tacit disappointment.

Uncle Jack's house
From time to time, Mum would take me to Uncle Jack's house. I was 'got ready' in my outdoor clothes, and my mother and I would walk, or after I had the infamous tricycle, ride and walk, down Wherret's Well Lane, past the house with the high dark green hedges that always reminded me of Christmas, round into Lugtrout Lane. My Uncle Jack's was along here, past the sugar beet field on the right, and the football field on the left.

Uncle Jack's was set back from the road, a ramshackle farmhouse, red brick, with a drive but no gates. The house was on the left as you walked in to the drive, and beyond that, various animal pens. On the right were a number of greenhouses and sheds.

I did not go into the house as a rule, preferring to stay outside while my mother and Auntie Edie talked and had tea indoors.

Uncle Jack's was paradise. He had a smallholding, with all kinds of poultry, ducks, chickens, geese and rabbits. The rabbits were my favourites, they were of many different breeds, black and white Dutch, English blue chinchillas, Belgian hares, many ordinary brown ones and the most intriguing, a white one with pink eyes, which he told me was called an albino. I was fascinated by the albino, with its pink fleshed ears and soft dead-white fur. Sometimes Uncle Jack would get them out of the cages for me to hold. The rabbits were housed in a big wooden shed, with three sides, and the hutches were stacked two high along the sides, sheltered from the elements.

There were pigs, and nanny goats, in pens beyond the garden sheds. On one occasion there was a sow with piglets, and Uncle Jack lifted me up to see over the wooden door of the sty. The sow was lying down, an enormous pink animal with a hairy face, contentedly murmuring and snuffling, while the row of pink wriggling offspring tugged urgently at her teats, little squeals and grunts coming as they scrabbled and shifted against her side. We peered over the door and I could see the white of her eye as she swivelled her head to see us, without shifting her brood.

'Will she bite me?' I asked. Uncle Jack laughed.

'Oh yes, you mustn't go in there, she'd think you was a-goin for her babies and kill you.'

'Do all animals kill people who go for their babies?'

'Oh 'ar. I should think so' he said.

Uncle Jack made wreaths for funerals, and in the sheds he kept the tools of his trade. Wire for making up the shapes, circles and crosses, and quantities of moss. Sometimes he let me help, binding the ferns to the wire shapes, after he'd covered them with moss. At Christmas he'd make Christmas wreaths, with bright berried holly, red or yellow, ivy and sometimes laurel; and he always had a supply of mistletoe, which grew in profuse clumps in his apple trees.

Beyond the greenhouses and the sheds was Uncle Jack's vegetable plot. Neat and prolific, with flowers in the summer, dahlias and Sweet Williams, and an all round supply of fresh roots and leaves. Our family never suffered from food shortages during the war.

The greenhouses seemed huge, long and damp, with grimy glass and a warm, peaty, scent. I loved going in there. Uncle Jack wore thick dark grimy trousers which were redolent of the greenhouses. He grew ferns, and pointed out the different types, maidenhair, filmy, and sturdier sorts, rows upon rows in their orange-brick pots, lined up on staging below which were empty pots together with dusty bags made of sacking. They smelled rich, pungent and earthy.

'What are they, Uncle Jack?'

'Oh, that's bonemeal, and that's blood and fishmeal. Fertiliser, like food, for the plants, makes them grow.'

'Like our food?'

'That's right, like the rabbits.'

'I like rabbit' I said, thinking of my mother's rabbit stew. Wild rabbit was plentiful then, and cheap.

'Do you want one to take home with you?'

'Ooh, can I have that white one?'

'You can have one of the black and white ones, but we'll have to ask Dad to make a pen for it, first.'

My mother said I could have the black and white rabbit, and that was settled. I was thrilled to be getting a rabbit, and only marginally upstaged when my mother told me, on the way home, that Uncle Jack had given my brother a nanny goat to bring home when he was little, like me.

My dad's office
My dad's office was a small building of tongue and groove boarding with a tiled pitched roof. It was painted green, with a sign over the door which read A.H. Proctor Ltd. Unusually, it featured a fireplace but quite where the smoke escaped I

never found out.

My dad was a coal merchant, or rather he was the office clerk-cum-manager of A. H. Proctor, Coal and Coke Factors. He sold every imaginable type of solid fuel, coal, coke, peat blocks. There was nutty slack, best nuts, ovoids. I loved ovoids; they had a lovely name, a name you could say over and over again like a mantra. They were egg shaped smooth moulded objects with a flat bit around the middle. They were satisfyingly filthy, comfortable to hold and fitted my little hands perfectly.

The office was at the station end of a large yard, by the railway sidings, and it was a great adventure to run up and down the yard, looking at the heaps of shiny coal and coke. Dad's office was wonderful; a small crammed dark wooden shed with, surprisingly, a fireplace. There was a roaring fire in winter. My dad had a chair and a desk, under the window. There was another chair for customers and visitors, a plain armless wooden one with a seat made of dark green leatherette where I could sit; but my dad's chair was best, with a rounded back and wooden spindles like the bars of a cot; and a cushion, greyed and flat with age. When Dad had to go out of the office for any reason I was allowed to sit in his chair, to be a good girl and mind the office. My feet could not touch the ground, but I could see over the top of the desk, and out through the window, and I felt very important indeed. My dad's office smelt of wood, and paper, and smoke. Sometimes it smelt of tobacco. I loved the smell of his tobacco, moist and woody, dark shag, it was called, which made me laugh. There were a million things to look at and investigate: staples and paperclips; ink, pencils; rubber bands; indelible pencils which you could lick and turn into purplish-blue ink, like magic. The indelible pencils stained my lips and tongue. There were huge ledgers, with dark leather bindings and columns full of my dad's neat writing and figures.

Fostered
It was on one of these expeditions to the office that my dad told me that I was going to stay with my Auntie Turner, and Uncle Bert. I had never heard of Auntie Turner, or Uncle Bert

but I had no reason to question their existence. When Uncle Bert turned up one day at the station, with his bicycle, it never occurred to me to resist, or to wonder why I had a small suitcase; I simply accepted that this was how it was to be, and taking his hand obediently, walked away from my dad and towards my new home.

My first day at school

Norah, our refugee, was lovely. A cheerful and kind lady, who made me laugh and who spent time with me, taking me for walks and so on. She was always smiling. Norah was a saviour in many ways. I was always pleased to see her. So pleased in fact, that on my very first day at school, as I processed in a crocodile with the other children from the reception class at the end of the school day, I was unable to contain myself and broke ranks from the sedate two-by-two column and rushed towards the school gates yelling 'Auntie Norah, Auntie Norah', at the top of my voice. It was I suppose a seminal moment in my school career. The teacher halted the crocodile and ran to the gates, catching up with me before I reached them. Under the fascinated gaze of assorted mothers and my newly acquired classmates, I was stopped in my tracks. The teacher held my arm very firmly, and told me, in a loud voice, that that was NOT the way to behave, and that I must walk, with the other children, until we reached the gates. I was turned around and dragged, crying, back towards the crocodile, placed in my original position, and only then was order restored and we were allowed to continue down the playground. It was my first taste of humiliation by teacher.

School milk

At playtime there was milk to be drunk. I loathed the milk. It was stacked outside the door of our classroom, several crates high, to sit in the morning sun until it acquired a faintly 'off' taste, slightly warm, with a stiff layer of cream, firm under the silver top of each small bottle. I learned that I need not drink it. We were unsupervised for the purpose of milk drinking and I rapidly realised that I could barter my bottle of milk in exchange for friendship. The usual recipient of this was a large chubby boy called Nigel Wiggins.

Pauline Hamilton

Pauline is also a creative writing student. She is thinking about writing her life story but has started by summing up part of her life in a concise extract (below), which she may then use as a starting point to write something longer.

They say convent girls are the worst; they become wild children on the rebound. I was not a convent girl but I had suffered eight long years incarcerated in a famous girls' public school while my parents enjoyed the delights of the British Raj out east. All my teenage years wasted on dry as dust subjects – maths, Latin, medieval history—and in the end I had failed my Oxford Entrance exam. My father was disgusted:

'You might as well go to Art School. I'm not paying any more fees to that place.'

I was a pretty girl. I went to Art School like a lamb to the slaughter, lost my virginity at a wild party in the first term and chalked up one-night stands like there was no tomorrow. Parties, parties, parties! It was 1954 and London was like a magnet to us. The Chelsea Arts Ball, the Diaghilev Exhibition, the French pub in Dean Street; years of burning the candle at both ends; all hidden from my parents. Every weekend I returned home as a demure Miss Joan Hunter Dunn and played tennis with the vicarage family. My father had now retired and remarried; he had a respectable property in a Home Counties village. Showing me my new bedroom, he told me:

'Look out of this window, Pauline. There's the village green and there's the war memorial. Do you see that church? That's where I am going to lead you down the aisle on your wedding day, and this, this is the very mirror you will use to try on your wedding dress. . .'

I can remember a sick feeling of revulsion at the whole idea. I hardly knew my father after years of separation, let alone the Scotswoman he had married. My mother had died out in Rangoon and left me £5000. I resolved to go abroad.

So that is how, in 1957, I travelled to the island of Ibiza. In those days the island was sunk in poverty with only a mailboat every three weeks, no airport, no paved roads and no electricity. I bought an old boat with a lateen rig and went sailing with a handsome fisherman who spoke a bit of French. We sailed right round the island, putting in at beautiful deserted beaches and cooking the fish we caught on driftwood fires.

One day I was talking to a Canadian couple I knew, Rolf and Mary; they said:

'It's so beautiful here. We want to find a way to live here permanently.'

In that moment an idea was born. I was 23 years old and sick of London life. I knew I wanted to settle down and start having a family. Neither the chinless subalterns produced by my father nor the cynical roués I had been to bed with in London were husband material in my book.

'Vicente, voulez-vous marier avec moi?' I asked my fisherman friend.

'Bien sur! OK! Pourquois pas!'

Nothing in my life had prepared me for the storm that now hit us. I had written a naïve letter to my dad full of excitement at the wonderful news. It was received with blind fury and he announced his imminent arrival. He had been to see his MP about it and spoken on the phone to the British Consul in Palma in an attempt to ban the marriage.

'Spain is not Europe!' he declared. 'I'm not having a bloody dago for a son-in-law.'

When the day came for his arrival, we went to meet him off the ship. Vicente's mother had come to greet her new relative and stood by the gangplank: a little old lady dressed in black from head to foot. My dad slowly descended the gangplank, dressed in a city suit, a Homburg hat, a briefcase and a furious scowl. Vicente and I stepped forward to greet him but he strode straight past us towards his hotel. Then he turned and called me to follow him.

I had been brought up with no money-consciousness and no idea of how the world works. It was a revelation to me that my father assumed I was the victim of hustlers.

'Are you pregnant?'

'No, but I wish I was.'

A sigh of relief from him:

'This is what I am going to do. The Bishop of Ibiza has agreed to block the marriage under a local law for three months. Because you are 23 I can't stop it for more than that, but I hope you'll come to your senses by then.'

I remember feeling so outraged by his behaviour that I decided then and there that, even if I hadn't really felt that bothered, I was definitely going ahead now.

The next day we went with my father to visit the family home. Vicente tried to talk to him in French but he pretended not to understand. When we got to the little whitewashed house in the fields his sister brought out simple rush-bottomed chairs for us to sit on and drew ice-cold water from the well which she poured in glasses for us.

That was all 53 years ago, and last year I went back to Ibiza with Vicente's and my daughter Lili and her teenage daughter Lucy and we walked through the same fields, which are now studded with hotels. We visited Pepita, my ex-sister-in-law and she is now rich and prosperous: I wonder if she ever thinks of that day.

Of course the marriage didn't last but we had eight good years and two beautiful children. I have never regretted my trip to Ibiza.

ANNE ECKERSLEY
Anne is also a creative writing student of mine who chose to write about an important part of her life. She manages to combine humour, tension and lovely contemporary detail.

Four years, eleven months exactly

I was four years and eleven months old when I was first given my own room. I can be that precise even now because my cousin Simon is, and always has been, two years and a month older. And Uncle Peter, Aunty Pauline, Simon and Ian stayed the night with us before his seventh birthday.

We all slept in the back bedroom that night; at least the 'kiddywinks' did, as Uncle Peter liked to call us. It was much bigger than my new room whose pale pink flowery curtains matched the cushion on the chair. Sarah liked pink, which was lucky because it was going to be her room as soon as I moved into my new one. She was going to have to share it with Jane, but I guess she didn't know it then. Jane hadn't been born, but remembering Mother's swollen belly and candy-striped maternity wear, I guess she was well on her way.

I was allowed to choose the wallpaper myself. I went down to the decorator's shop in town with Father. They had enormous books, so heavy that Father had to hold them as I turned the pages. I had to sit on a high stool but I considered every single page, very carefully indeed, even if in the end the choice was easy.

Father had finished hanging my Magic Roundabout paper long before they arrived, but my newly painted, deep dusky pink, glossed doors still had to dry. There was that bitter synthetic smell I still associate with wallpaper paste, the one that hits the back of your nose, which combined with fresh paint fumes was a smell any self-respecting four-year-old, nearly five-year-old, would do well to avoid. I slept in the back room too.

Sarah and I were supposed to share a mattress on the floor and Ian and Simon Sarah's bed. I doubt any of us stayed where we were put. I'd lay money we'd have all ended up on the mattress on the floor within minutes, listening to our bedtime story, giggling and fighting for space.

I forget what the story was. I couldn't have concentrated anyway; I had something far more important on my mind. I knew a secret I wasn't allowed to tell anyone. Uncle Peter had sworn me to secrecy. He said I mustn't even tell my teddy, because teddies weren't good at keeping secrets. I probably had to cross my heart. I don't think he would have made me hope to die, Mother wouldn't have liked that and Uncle Peter always looked as if he was a little bit frightened of her.

He told me what Simon's birthday present was going to be and I did keep the secret. I didn't tell anyone, especially not Simon. Teddy even slept alone in our new room just in case he guessed.

At some point that night I asked Simon what he wanted for his birthday and what he'd do if he had all the money in the world. He said he'd buy guns. He just wanted guns for his birthday and stuff to make bombs with. He said if I knew what his present was, he would have to shoot me.

I said how.

He said he'd shoot me with the biggest gun he got tomorrow, so I knew he didn't have a clue.

Ian and Sarah fought, they always did. They looked angelic and were both so blond everyone thought they were more closely related than they are. Simon and I looked similar too apparently because Mother said people struggled to tell us apart in our baby photos even if he was my cousin not my brother.

In those days we both had dark hair and brown eyes. Simon said I copied him because he was older than me. I said I didn't and he said I was lying so he'd have to shoot me tomorrow anyway.

He didn't.

Jane will be mousy, but she hasn't arrived yet, she wasn't even due for another six weeks at that point. A September baby, an overenthusiastically celebrated Christmas party conception but the reason I'm getting my own room. I hoped she'd be a boy. I would have really liked an elder brother like Geoffrey or John, even an older sister. It was just such a big responsibility being the eldest child. People tell you all sorts of things.

Eventually the following morning came, I don't remember when Simon was told his birthday present was going to be a few months on a ship and the rest of his life in a foreign land.

'I'm going to where they grow bananas,' he told me, matter-of-factly, as his dad put their suitcases into our car. I can't remember whether or not he was pleased about it. He didn't get any guns anyway. I wouldn't have been pleased if I was him. Not because I wanted guns, but I'd never given much thought to where bananas grow but I knew you could get them easily enough at the local market.

However, we took them to Southampton to catch their ship. We all crowded into our white Vauxhall Victor Super. Mother, heavily pregnant, sat in the back with all of the children and a tin of Quality Street. We didn't usually have sweets in the car, in case we were sick. The only exception I can remember was the journey home after summer holidays with Auntie Pamela. Auntie Doris next door, without fail, the moment we had all got into the car, would come running down her path, waving madly – 'I'm so glad I caught you,' and give us a box of Meltis Newberry Fruits for the journey home. They were and still are my favourites.

But on the journey to the docks on that warm July day, those who were sitting in the back adopted Father's system. 'One forward, one back,' he ordered, and we'd seat ourselves in a tightly packed, fan-like arrangement whilst in spacial luxury on the red-leather front seat sat the three grown ups. Father drove, Uncle Peter was navigator. Auntie Pauline sat between them.

We weren't sick, any of us, but then Mother ate most of the chocolates. She said it was her hormones.

'Hormones! Now there is a frightening word,' laughed Uncle Peter. And I laughed too because I didn't think anybody could be frightened of a word that meant you could eat chocolate whenever you wanted.

We stood on the edge of the dock until their ship had sailed away, Father said he could see them all waving goodbye so we should wave back. Mother couldn't see them and went and sat in the car with the chocolates, but Father said we had to keep waving because it didn't matter whether or not we could see them, they could still see us. So we all waved hard until the ship sailed out of the harbour entrance and was out of sight.

We went to drive away but the car got stuck in the railway lines. Mother said it was Father's fault – he should've looked where he was going before he parked there.

'Thank you darling,' he said, raising his eyebrows. 'For stating the bleeding obvious.' He went for help and came back with some blocks of wood, while Mother, Sarah and I sat in the back, waiting and eating chocolates. I suspect Mother ate all the long thin yellow ones and the green triangles. She always did even when her hormones weren't a problem.

Father did something with the wooden blocks and managed to drive the car over the lines and away.

Mother said it was lucky the line wasn't used anymore because otherwise we'd all be electrocuted. I don't remember what Father said, but Mother started singing loudly and pointing at us.

We visited the *HMS Victory*, on the way home. 'Anyone who died on board ship,' the matronly woman told us, 'would have been sewn into a canvas shroud. And for good measure, the final stitch would be pushed through the nose to make sure they were well and truly dead.' And then providing the shrouded body didn't wake up suddenly and scream "leave my nose alone", they would be thrown over the side to spend eternity floating about in the sea.' Sarah cried all the way home because she didn't think Ian had looked well, or that she'd ever see him again with or without a hole in his nose. She didn't, but he got there safely enough, they all did. They just never came back.

We pinned a map of the world on the board in the kitchen and every time we had a postcard or letter, we'd move a red drawing pin along the shaky pencil line Mother had drawn, so we knew how far they still had to go.

I guess eventually one or other of us pressed the pin into Australia, but by then we'd probably lost interest. Soon after the map disappeared anyway, probably hidden by the sea of school notes, babysitting rotas, recipes and bills that formed part of normal daily life and had to be stored somewhere for safekeeping.

Jane came along six weeks later and I didn't eat bananas for ages. I can't remember what my seventh birthday present was, apart from a ten shilling note from Auntie Kit – Christmas and birthdays always meant the same token was forthcoming, even post-decimalisation. Just that I had another two years of worry before I realised I didn't need to go anywhere. And I didn't. Possibly that's why – years of childhood stress and unresolved trauma later – I still live only three miles away from where I was born.

Years later I told my parents how worried I'd been. The caring people they are, they just laughed.

'You were always a worrier,' Mother said. 'We would never have gone there, they have man eating spiders there.'

'Hmph!' said Father. 'We didn't need to. We've always paid all our bills on time, why on earth should we have done a moonlight-flit?'

My War

The following extract is taken from the diary of Wiliam Siggery who spelt his first name with one 'l'. He was born in 1910 and died in 1952. His nephew Peter kindly lent us part of his diary which makes fascinating reading and gives a great insight into the Second World War. Wiliam returned safely and went on to get married and have three children.

I had almost completed my four years in the Army when war broke out in 1939 and I was called to colours. I went into training at Tidworth, then Aldershot in preparation for a tour of duty in France. In January 1940, with all the village people cheering us off, we set out for France and the Belgian border.

Things were quiet until May when Jerry started his push into Belgium. I was the Guard Commander the night we had our first air-raid warning. That night we slept in our boots expecting to be moved. But when the push came, the guard was left until last. I could see Jerry dive bombing the other end of town.

We lay flat in a side street with bombs dropping around us. A youngster screamed. I ran out. Catching him, I covered him with my tin hat, lying beside him until the coast was clear. Above us our fighters came to our rescue bringing down two German planes.

We waited about dining on bully and biscuits, while the French treated us to wine and more biscuits, until about five in the afternoon when there was a roar of planes overhead and a rattle of machine gunfire. A good old dog fight was in progress. I saw two of our own shot down and a third flew overhead, Jerry on his tail.

Our C.O. decided we should move and we set off – a convoy of thirty lorries along roads packed with refugees. Young and old crammed into both cars and horse drawn wagons while those who could not get onto the wagons walked behind. So many people, so few belongings, but they made our progress slow. As darkness fell we were bombed from all quarters. The sky lit up like a brilliant firework display. Hundreds must have been killed that night, it was a nightmare, but somehow our convoy escaped without damage and at dawn we arrived at St. Omer, where we immediately concealed ourselves in the woods.

We had a quiet day and an uncomfortable night cramped in a lorry trying to sleep on petrol tins. At nine the following morning we paraded and all those who had ever fired a 303 rifle were asked to fall out. Of over two hundred men, only twelve of us stepped forward. We were ordered to walk around and shoot at anything suspicious. Jerry tanks were reportedly heading our way, so we barricaded the gates and a man was posted every twelve yards or so. But suddenly, with the Jerry tanks in view, the gunfire stopped and they moved off in another direction.

We stuck to our posts and watched another terrific dogfight overhead. But then we heard the roar of more planes. Dozens of them, dropping bombs everywhere. But luck, it seemed, was again on our side – we suffered no damage.

As evening came, the Sergeant Major told us we needed to remain on guard all night. Apart from a nightingale singing in the trees near me, it was a lonely job. At midnight I heard the whuff of a long range gun and the whizz of a shell which crashed into the town. Jerry kept that up for three hours, until he had smashed up the whole town. But the nightingale sang on.

We moved out about four in the morning and made good progress until our despatch riders returned with the news, Jerry tanks ahead were blocking the road. We turned off and ended up hiding ourselves in the wooded grounds of a large house. The rain that day and the small dinner rations did nothing to cheer our spirits.

After dinner I sat under a tree, hugging my rifle between my knees and fell asleep. I was awakened by the terrific report from a gun. Grabbing my rifle, I released the safety catch, pulled back the bolt, only to find it was jammed. Someone had taken my rifle while I was asleep and left me with just a dud.

Jerry was pumping lead into those woods. To my relief I found my own rife and rushed to where the firing was coming from. Chaps were rushing everywhere, they told me to be careful – our own sergeants were firing on anything that moved. Luckily they were poor marksmen or some of our men would have copped a packet.

I went to where the firing was coming from but I could see nothing. Jerry was well hidden. It was suicide standing there. One fellow after another went down. I had forty rounds of ammunition, not a lot.

One of our chaps took a look round the house. He shot a French Officer when he didn't obey the 'Halt' command. The man was our interpreter.

When the death was reported to our C.O. he just nodded. 'Be more careful next time,' he said.

Everyone got into places where they could have a go at Jerry. There was a convoy some distance off, but neither I nor an officer with field glasses could make out who it was. Someone volunteered to go off on a motorcycle to find out. He never returned, nor did two other chaps who took a lorry to find out. The decision was made – we should move out.

Throwing supplies out of the lorries we made room for the wounded and dead. No one wanted to leave them behind. But setting off at full speed we ignored the French people who beckoned us to go back and we drove straight into the trap prepared for us. Jerry had blown our first lorry up. It blocked the road. But even if it had not, we couldn't have got much further. The railway crossing gates were down. A gun positioned in front of them.

Nothing for it, we jumped out, diving into the woods. Twelve of us hid behind some bushes. Machine guns and rifle fire was going on all around us so we couldn't move from our hiding place without walking straight into a hail of bullets. We waited. We had to. The suspense was terrible. I was on look-out but the other chaps said,

'Lay down Sigs, we are whacked.'

I told them I had to have a go first, that I would rather be killed than be taken. Crawling out of the bushes on my hands and knees I spotted three Jerrys coming through the trees. I knelt up, about to raise my rifle, but too late. Ping – I felt a pain in my chest and went down. My mates, seeing what had happened, threw their arms up and let Jerry line them up and go through their pockets.

A Jerry officer saw me lying there and asked one of our chaps to put a field dressing on me. I asked for some water and a Jerry guard threw his bottle over. I drained it.

We stayed there until a crowd of German soldiers came past. They marched the others off, but the two of them who brought up the rear were carrying me. They took us into the station and laid me down on the platform. A Jerry came over with two cushions for me to lie on and I thanked him. Another asked me how I felt. He said my wound was not bad and would soon heal.

An officer came up and asked two of our chaps to help dress the French who had been wounded. They did and brought them over. They were in a bad way. Another officer came along; and speaking English ordered them to fall in with the Germans, but asked one comrade to stay with me.

A young chap said, 'shall I stay with you?'

I said, 'I wish you would.' And with that I said cheerio to the others. They were marched off into the night. What became of them after that I have no idea for I was so tired, what with the loss of blood and lack of sleep, I soon forgot everything and fell asleep.

I awoke the next morning to find my mate still sitting at my feet wide awake. Everywhere was quiet. I looked around and saw the wounded French next to me were dead. We were taken that day to the First Aid post in town run by the French Medical Corps where we met another chap who recognised me. My two comrades were sent away in a lorry. I wanted to go with them but was not allowed.

While I was lying on a stretcher outside the ambulance a French woman from one of the houses opposite put a peppermint into my mouth and a bag full of them in my pocket. I thanked her profusely, I was so dry.

The Germans moved me to a barn full of injured Frenchmen within a German camp. It was dark, hot, stuffy and smelt of blood. Rats ran over everything and everyone, even sniffing our faces. I suppose they could smell blood. I decided to escape as soon as I could and with that thought on my mind fell asleep.

My chance came the following day, I was told to go outside with some of the less injured French and we walked about. Jerry too busy to pay us any close attention. I made a dive for the high hedge and went over it with a bit of difficulty. There was a farm house on the other side of the field, I went as quickly as I could trying not to give myself away.

I owe my freedom to the kind folks there. They gave me food and while I was eating the farmer came in with a pair of trousers and a jacket. He said I wouldn't get far in my uniform. He was right, so I let them dress me as a refugee wearing a beret and carrying a bag filled with straw to look like a valise.

I plodded across fields and down country roads, avoiding towns, going round them the best way I could. No one took notice of me, there were plenty just the same on the roads. Jerry even passed me without a second look, that gave me confidence.

At one point I took shelter in a ditch, seeing the smoke from an eighteen pounder, hearing the whizz, then the bang and feeling the spray of earth as it fell not far from me. It was my intention to head for Calais. After an early start next morning I was not sure of my way. In my best French I asked a fellow on the road. He looked at me and said 'You English soldier?' I shook my head, but he rushed into a nearby house and came out with two more men. They started calling after me. Perhaps they wanted to help, I didn't take a chance and ran. Eventually they gave up but I knew I had to watch my step.

At one point after I had been walking for hours I had a close encounter. There were two abandoned refugee cars on the side of the road. I guess they had run out of petrol. Two German motorcycles appeared and stopped not far from me. Jerrys got off. My heart was in my mouth, but they went over to the cars and were looking them over and ignored me as I passed.

By the time I got onto the Calais Road, there were thousands of refugees retreating from Calais. I could see it in the distance; being bombed from all quarters, much of it going up in flames. I was on that road when something so distressing happened just ahead of me that I found myself completely unable to pass that spot. I turned round and retraced my steps.

Two kind women came to my rescue with eggs and coffee. They allowed me to wash and shave, but when I saw my reflection in the mirror I could scarcely believe it was me. I stayed a time talking to one of them. Her husband was in the army and she had not heard or seen him for a long time. I showed her a photo of my children. She asked me what I intended doing and I told her I was going to get through or die trying.

I needed to get back to where we had started and it would be better to do it in the dark. But that meant I needed to pass the German camps and the men who had chased me. I walked for about five hours, licking blades of grass when the thirst became too much. Eventually I got into a ditch, climbing into my sack and using the straw as a pillow I lay there thinking about everybody back home and whether I would see them again. I got all my photos out and studied them. Tears came and I cried so much I was trembling like a leaf, my teeth chattering. I wasn't cold, but my nerves were giving way. I wanted to scream, I felt like I was going mad. I just wanted a bomb to fall on me and put an end to my misery. People passed me from time to time and I shook even more, worried Jerry would see me. The time dragged on, it didn't seem to get dark for ages. I lay there suffering in silence; I never want to go through anything like that again.

Every farm I passed had a dog that would start barking. I had to cross two streams, more mud and slime than water. The Jerrys kept coming and the machine guns kept up their fire until I didn't know which way the bullets were coming from. I crawled on hands and knees, wearing out my trousers. By the time I swam across a canal, I was finished, totally exhausted. I knew Jerry was watching me and I expected at any moment to feel a bullet in my back but I didn't care.

When I reached a burning village, my first thought was to get warm. I found a house, its back burnt out and I went in. Shutting the door up, it felt like a furnace so I took off all my clothes and laid them drying while I warmed myself. When the roof over the front part collapsed it was time to move on.

Another stream, more fields and I finally came to a town that was barricaded up. I was stopped at the point of a bayonet, but they were French soldiers on guard and when I showed them my identity disks they took me to an old school room and a man who spoke English with a bottle of whisky. I drank quickly but it was too much for me and I collapsed only to wake an hour later to find Jerry was shelling the town. These French men got me back to Dunkirk, although the journey there was fast, furious and definitely not for the faint hearted. We didn't arrive a moment too soon, men were swimming out to the boats and Jerry was bombing the coast. I asked what was happening and was told we were evacuating as we were surrounded.

By Tuesday the last food I'd eaten was on Saturday. One of the officers went out to see if we could get away, but he came back four hours later with the news that the boats were full. However there was a chance for the following day, we should be ready at nine the next morning.

I was feeling rotten with hunger and walked all over the place to see if I could get anything to eat. I spotted a piece of bread and jam on a stretcher and pounced on it. I saw it was covered in blood but that didn't matter. I was hungry so down it went. I did enjoy it and should have liked more.

We got up early the next morning and put all the stretcher cases outside ready for them to be picked up. Then the officer came round and said, 'I am sorry boys, they can't take us today.'

My heart sank. But he told those of us who could walk we could go down the beach. Twelve of us set off leaving those poor chaps behind. I don't know if they got away in time. Off we went, meeting a chap in a pair of shorts with a smashed foot. I and another chap carried him between us. 'Don't leave me,' he said and we didn't. It was hard work lugging him with us on empty stomachs but it was even more painful for him. About half way along, I spotted a bike and ran over to get it; we put him on and pushed him the remainder of the way.

Those last three days were hell, but that day walking six miles along the beach didn't seem so bad. The beaches were littered with rifles, respirators and complete kits the chaps had thrown down so they could swim for it.

I reached the boat, but it was a job for me to get on because they didn't know whom I was. But once on board they gave me tea and told me we were sailing for England, I couldn't believe it.

At Margate the police, took me for a spy and questioned me. They must have believed me eventually because they took me to the ARP depot and then to Westminster Hospital in London. It was there I had a bath, a meal and was given a clean bed. They contacted May and she came the next day.

I convalesced at Sutton Emergency Hospital for about six months before I was discharged both from hospital and the army.

And eventually I went back to my work at Huntley and Palmers in Reading.

Useful contacts

Self-publishing:

www.lulu.com
www.authorhouse.co.uk

The Book Guild
Book Guild Publishing Ltd
Pavilion View
19 New Road
Brighton
East Sussex
BN1 1UF
01273 720900

Source for buying old papers from your early life:
www.Historic-Newspapers.co.uk.

Sources for timelines:
www.bbc.co.uk/history
www.timelineuk.com

Index